linguistiss

ENGLISH LINGUISTICS
1500—1800

(A Collection of Facsimile Reprints)

Selected and Edited by
R. C. ALSTON

No. 322

THE SCOLAR PRESS LIMITED
MENSTON, ENGLAND
1972

JOSEPH WEBBE

LESSONS AND EXERCISES
OUT OF CICERO

1627

A Scolar Press Facsimile

THE SCOLAR PRESS LIMITED
MENSTON, ENGLAND
1972

THE SCOLAR PRESS LIMITED
20 Main Street, Menston, Yorkshire, England

SBN 85417 669 1

Printed in Great Britain by
The Scolar Press Limited
Menston, Yorkshire, England

NOTE

Reproduced (original size) by permission of the Librarian of St. Mary's Vicar's Library, Marlborough.

Joseph Webbe's importance in the history of English linguistics has already been signified in volumes 42 and 74 in this series, and in an article by Vivian Salmon in *The Library* (1961, pp. 190-96). The present work was designed in conformity with the *Pueriles Confabulatiunculae* published in the same year. It was printed on one side of the paper only though in this facsimile this particular feature has been dispensed with.

Copies of the original are rare—only four being recorded. None of Webbe's works have been previously reprinted. This title is not recorded in *STC*.

LESSONS

AND

EXERCISES

Out of

CICERO AD ATTICVM,

FOR SVCH AS DESIRE TO
habituate themfelues (either by their owne
induſtry, or by the helpe of Maſters) in
Cicero's *epiſtolarie Latine,*

After the Method of D. WEBBE,

Lately priuiledged by Patent from his
MAIBSTIE for 31. yeeres.

*And are to be ſold by euery Maſter licenſed to teach by
that way.*

As by M. Sherley *in Roſe-alley, at the vpper end of
Holborne, towards Grayes-Inne Fields.*

M. Clarke *in Fetter-lane, now teaching at the Church
of* S. *Dunſtane in the Weſt.*

M. Waſtell *in Harpe-lane, at the further end of the
Church of* S. *Dunſtane in the Eaſt, and others.*

Imprinted at London by *F. K.*
An. Domini 1627.

Ĵm°. Chr.
L.1.C.12.

BOnum nobis est, quòd patiamur quandoq; contradictores, & quòd malè & imperfectè de nobis sentiatur, etiamsi benè agimus & intendimus. Ista sæpè iuuant ad humilitatem, & à vana gloria nos defendunt. Tunc enim meliùs interiorem testem Deum quærimus, quando foris vilipendimur ab hominibus, & non benè nobis creditur.

READER.

N my Petition to the Parliament, I made mention of a twofold vſe of Authors reduced vnto my method. The one was of enabling a man preſently to write his own conceit, in his Authors ſtile and Latine, or other languages ſo reduced. Which though it may ſtand ſuch in great ſtead, as haue no leiſure to breed an habit of ſpeaking or writing the tongue that they would vſe : yet it cannot preſently bee called their own, by reaſon that what they write, they write within booke.

The other vſe was of breeding an habit in the learners ; and of making thereby any Authors language their owne language : For by this, they write and ſpeake (according to the proportion of their reading) as pure as he doth, and that very readily and without booke.

Both theſe vſes, though they be of great moment. Yet the later ſooneſt makes vs greateſt proficients. And therfore I am firſt falne vpon it:

and

and to this end haue claufed this piece of *Cic. ad Attic.* for the vfes of our fchooles.

Wherin I defire thee only at this prefent to take notice of two forts of claufes; the one fimple, th'other compounded, inuolued, or intermingled : yet for thy eafier and more profitable vfe, wee haue vntyed the knot of thefe inuolued claufes, and reduced them to their fimplicitie : but fo, that by certaine calling markes or figures, thou mayft giue euery one their proper places.

And thefe marked, or figured, may be alfo called pregnant claufes, as, (being reduced to their proper reading, and inuoluing) they carry other claufes in their bellies.

For example, let vs take (a.1.1.61.) that is the threefcore and fixth claufe, of the firft Epiftle, of the firft book, of *Cicero ad Atticum.* Where a. is the Volume; the firft 1. the booke of that volume; the fecond 1. the Epiftle of that booke; and 61. the claufe of that Epiftle.

This claufe is thus written, *Nos* (a.1.1.61.a.) *fummam adhibebimus diligentiam.* And the claufe reprefented by that (a.1.1.61.a) (wherein the later a. doth but diftinguifh the firft 61. from the fecond,) followes thus:

In omni munere candidatorio fungendo. Which though it be an entire fimple claufe, and is now ready fitted for fome further occafion: yet confidering thefe two, but as one inuolued claufe, this laft is out of his naturall place. And in true reading of your Author fhould bee fet where it

is

is appointed or called by his figures in the firſt clauſe in this manner: *Nos in omni munere Canditatorio fungendo, ſummam adhibebimus diligentiam.* And according to this ſimple placing, they haue many times their pointing ; which may ſeeme prepoſterous, but is not, as being already eaſily reconciled.

Becauſe we talke ſo much of clauſes, it may bee thou wilt aske vs what we meane by a clauſe. I'le tell thee. We call a clauſe, a perfect member of ſpeech, conſiſting of one or moe words rightly knit vnto other members, either before, or after, or both before and after. Which being broken off in any other part than in his true ioynt or knitting, breeds a fracture and diſorder in thy future Exerciſes, and compoſitions ; as ſhall hereafter more fully appeare in *Eulogio noſtro formali.*

Theſe Clauſes thou art to keepe entire ; and to let euery word haue his owne place, as well in Engliſh, as in Latine : but eſpecially in the Latine, which thou wilt finde thy ſelfe more able to performe than in the Engliſh: In that the meaning of the Engliſh & Latine being all one, thou art, as being Maſter of thine own tongue, able to vary the words of the Engliſh clauſe by a ſundry expreſſion of one and the ſame meaning ; which thou art not ſo wel able, as yet, to alter in the Latine.

And thinke not that we (though wee haue put an Engliſh interpretation to euery clauſe) are ſo fond as to ſuppoſe that no man can giue other

engliſhes,

englishes, or better than ours are, for these clauses. Our intent is, to figure and reprefent the true meaning of that claufe in Latine ; and the meaning being but one, if the englifh fit that meaning, be it what it wil(fo it be not barbarous) we are contented.

Other vfes of thefe bookes, wee leaue to the fore-named Mafters : who as faithfull ftewards to ancient Authors, and their vfe and cuftome may by their daily practice not onely direct thee for the prefent: but alfo finde out more hereafter than thou or I haue euer thought of.

This booke we haue diuided into pages or leffons: And after them we haue annexed fome Exercifes, which may plainely fhew vs the profits that children and all other forts of learners may weekely make, after the firft moneths teaching, by this or any other booke reduced to this method. And ere long wee will giue thee a Grammaticall practice vpon this booke, for the further fatisfaction of fuch as are not contented to call cuftome and Authoritie a reafon, but will haue a Grammar rule, the onely reafon of fpeaking or writing languages. Though the graueft and moft learned Iudges in this cafe haue already determined, that no reafon can giue rule to fpeech, but vfe and cuftome, from whence all petty rules and reafons are deriued: Yea, and though their owne wiues, daughters and fifters, are found by vfe and cuftome to fpeake as good Englifh as the greateft fchollers, and yet neuer knew Datiue or Ablatiue,

latiue, Prefent or Future, Noune or Verbe, or other English Collections, or curiofities.

As thefe women fpeake, fo fpeake our fchollers: the women fpeake good Englifh by vfe and cuftome; and our fchollers by the fame vfe and cuftome fpeake as good, if not better Latine, as comming from waryer and wifer authoritie. And fhall we yet thinke that both thefe fpeake like Parrots? Let vs take heed, lest wee that are fo great pretenders in this kind of vulgar learning, be not at legth out-faced by the arguments of boyes and women.

I neuer was againft the Grammar: for I purpofe, mine owne children (if God grant them life) fhall learne it, but not vntill they haue in fome meafure the language. For by that time they will not onely with their riper yeeres haue riper iudgements to conceiue fo hard a Theorie as that of Grammar: but will beforehand bee well acquainted with that fubiect whereof it treateth.

And as in the defcription of a City or Country, it is a far greater helpe vnto that Readers vnderftanding, to haue liued within it, & furueyed euery part of it; than to his that was neuer there, & is fain to frame vnto himfelfe fome extrauagant & phantaftick Idol, according vnto his vnexperienced conceipt therof: fo, doubtleffe, is it far eafier for an Italian to learn an Italian Grammar; or a Frenchman to learne a French Grammar; than for a raw Englifh or Dutchman, that is altogether vnacquainted with thefe tongues, to learne eyther of them; and no doubt but they fhall farre fooner,

with

with greater eafe, and more vnderftandingly learn
it, than he fhall euer learne it till he hath that language. Can this bee true in French or Italian
Grammars, and not in the Latine? it were impof-
fible. Now then let me tell you, that our habitua-
ted fchollers will in language be good Latines,
therefore fhould fooner, eafier, and with greater
iudgement learne that Grammar, than thofe of
what yeeres or capacitie foeuer, that neuer knew
a word of that language; therefore much more
than children, whofe tender wits and yeeres are
very vnfit to vndergoe fo heauy burdens. But (I
hope) the practice of our fchooles fhall end this
Controuerfie; efpecially when by that Grammaticall practice, they fhall find, that rules fhall runne
along with Authoritie. And when by that fup-
plement(which I haue fpoken of in my Petition,)
they may to any fenfe fupply thofe words that fhall
be wanting in their prefent Authors.

CICERO

ATTICO

S.

Touching our ſute,	a. 1.	1.	1.	PEtitionis noſtræ,
whereof I know you very carefull ;	a. 1.	1.	2.	quam tibi ſummæ cura eſſe ſcio,
this is the ſtate,	a. 1.	1.	3.	huiuſmodi ratio eſt,
ſo farre as hitherto	a. 1.	1.	4.	quod adhuc
may be coniectu- red.	a. 1.	1.	5.	coniectura prouide- ri poſsit.
Publius Galba one- ly ſolliciteth,	a. 1.	1.	6.	Prenſat vnus P. Gal- ba,
without colour or deceit,	a. 1.	1.	7.	ſine fuco ac fallacijs,
after the cuſtome of our Anceſtors.	a. 1.	1.	8.	more maiorum.
He is denied.	a. 1.	1.	9.	Negatur.
As 'tis thought,	a. 1.	1.	10.	Vt opinio eſt hominũ,
this his ouer-haſty negotiating was no hinderance to our proceeding ;	a. 1.	1.	11.	non aliena rationi noſtræ fuit illius hæc præpropera prenſatio ;
for	a. 1.	1.	12.	nam
they commonly ſo refuſe [him]	a. 1.	1.	13.	illi ita negant vulgo,
that they tell [him] they are in- gaged to me.	a. 1.	1.	14.	vt mihi ſe debere dicant.

So

So that	a. 1. 1. 15.	*Ita*
I hope fome bene-fit will accrew to vs,	a. 1. 1. 16.	*quiddam ſpero nobis profici,*
when this ſhall publikely be repor-ted,	a. 1. 1. 17.	*cùm hoc percrebreſ-cit,*
that there are ve-ry many found to fa-uour vs.	a. 1. 1. 18.	*plurimos noſtros a-micos inueniri.*
But	a. 1. 1. 19.	*(a.1.1.19.a.) Autem*
wee determined to begin to canuaſe or negotiat	a. 1. 1. 19.a	*nos (a.1.1.19.) initi-um prenſandi facere cogitaramus,*
at that very time	a. 1. 1. 20.	*eo ipſo tempore*
when	a. 1. 1. 21.	*quo*
Cincius ſaid, your ſeruant was ſetting out with theſe let-ters.	a. 1. 1. 22.	*tuum puerum cum hiſce literis proficiſci* Cincius *dicebat.*
In Campus [Mar-tius [or Mars-field]	a. 1. 1. 23.	*In Campo*
at the aſſembly for the choyce of Tribunes	a. 1. 1. 24.	*Comitijs tribunitijs*
on the ſixteenth of the Kalends of Auguſt.	a. 1. 1. 25.	*ad* a *XVI. Cal. Sext.*

a Ad deci-mum ſex-tum [diem] calend-rum Sextilis, vel kalendas Sextiles.

Com-

Competitors [about the Consulship] which were certainely difcerned [were] *Galba, Antonius,* and *Quintus Cornificius.*	a. 1.	1. 26.	*Competitores, qui çerti effe videbantur,* Galba [&] Antonius, & Qu. Cornificius.
I fuppofe	a. 1.	1. 27.	*Puto*
that at this you either laughed or grieued,	a. 1.	1. 28.	*te in hoc aut rififfe aut ingemuiffe,*
euen to the clapping of your forehead.	a. 1.	1. 29.	*vt frontem ferias.*
There are [fome]	a. 1.	1. 30.	*Sunt*
that thinke *Cafonius* [to be] alfo [a competitor.]	a. 1.	1. 31.	*qui etiam* Cæfonium *putent.*
Wee cannot imagine [that] *Aquilius* [puts for it]	a. 1.	1. 32.	Aquilium *non arbitramur,*
who refufeth [it,]	a. 1.	1. 33.	*qui denegat*
and	a. 1.	1. 34.	&
hath fworne he is not well,	a. 1.	1. 35.	*iurauit morbum,*
and	a. 1.	1. 36.	&

he

he hath excused himselfe vpon that same iurifdiction of his in ciuill Iudgements.	a. 1.	1. 37.	*illud fuum regnum iudiciale oppofuit.*
Catilina will affuredly be a Competitor,	a. 1.	1. 38.	Catilina (a. 1. 1. 38.a.) *certus erit competitor,*
when it fhall bee determined, that it is not light at noontide.	a. 1.	1. 38.a	*fi iudicatum erit meridie non lucére.*
About *Aufidius* and *Palicanus,*	a. 1.	1. 39.	*De* Aufidio & Palicano,
I cannot thinke you expect I fhould write vnto you.	a. 1.	1. 40.	*non puto te expectare dum fcribam.*
Of thofe	a. 1.	1. 41.	*Deys*
that are now in election,	a. 1.	1. 42.	*qui nunc petunt,*
Cæfar is thought certaine.	a. 1.	1. 43.	Cæfar *certus putatur.*
Thermus is held to contend with *Silanus* ;	a. 1.	1. 44.	Thermus *cum* Silano *contendere exiftimatur;*
who are fo poore	a. 1.	1. 45.	*qui fic inopes* (a.1. 1.45.a.) *funt,*
both in friends and efteeme,	a. 1.	1. 45.a	& *ab amicis* & *exiftimatione,*

that

that I thinke	a. 1.	1. 46.	*vt mihi videatur*
it not impoffible	a. 1.	1. 47.	*non effe ἀδύνατον*
to fet *Curius* a-gainft [them :]	a. 1.	1. 48.	Curium *obducere :*
but	a. 1.	1. 49.	*fed*
no man is of this opinion but my felf.	a. 1.	1. 50.	*hoc præter me nemini videtur.*
It feemeth to make very much for the furtherance of our affaires,	a. 1.	1. 51.	*Noftris rationibus maximè conducere videtur,*
that *Thermus* fhuld bee created [Confull[with *Cæfar :*	a. 1.	1. 52.	Thermum *fieri cum* Cæfare :
(for	a. 1.	1. 53.	(a. 1. 1. 53.a.)*enim*
there is not a man	a. 1.	1. 53.a	*Nemo eft*
of thofe	a. 1.	1. 53.b	*ex ijs*(a. 1. 1. 53.)
which now ftand,	a. 1.	1. 53.c	*qui nunc petunt,*
that is thought to be more fure to car-rie it.)	a. 1.	1. 54.	*qui* (a. 1. 1. 54. a) *firmior candidatus fore videatur.)*
if he fhall fortune to put for it in our yeare,	a. 1.	1. 54.a	*fi in noftrum annum reciderit,*
by reafon that	a. 1.	1. 55.	*propterea quòd*
he is ouerfeer for the repayring of the way *Flaminea.*	a. 1.	1. 56.	*Curator eft via Flaminia.*

which

Which when it shall be finished,	a. 1.	1. 57.	*Quæ cum erit abſoluta,*
then indeed will the Conſuls verie willingly ioyne him with *Cæſar.*	a. 1.	1. 58.	*ſanè facilè eum libentèr nunc* Cæſari *conſules addiderint.*
Of thoſe that ſtand [for the Conſulſhip]	a. 1.	1. 59.	*Petitorum*
this is [all] that I am hitherto informed.	a. 1.	1. 60.	*hæc eſt adhuc informata cogitatio.*
We will vſe all diligence,	a. 1.	1. 61.	*Nos* (a. 1. 1. 61. a.) *ſummam adhibebimus diligentiam,*
in performing the part of a candidate;	a. 1.	1. 61. a	*in omni munere candidatorio fungendo,*
and	a. 1.	1. 62.	*&*
it may be,	a. 1.	1. 63.	*fortaſſe,*
becauſe Gallia ſeemes to bee able to doe much	a. 1.	1. 64.	*quoniam videtur* (a. 1. 1. 64. a.) *multum poſſe Gallia*
in voyces,	a. 1.	1. 64. a	*in ſuffragijs,*
in the vacation at Rome	a. 1.	1. 65.	*Cum Romæ à iudicijs forum refrixerit,*
wee will goe Legats to Piſo	a. 1.	1. 66.	*excurremus* (a. 1. 1. 66. a.) *legati ad Piſonem,*
in September,	a. 1.	1. 66. a	*menſe Septembri,*
			that

3.

that wee may re-turne in Ianuarie.	a. 1. 1. 67.	*vt Ianuario reuertamur.*
When I shall perceiue how the Nobles are affected,	a. 1. 1. 68.	*Cùm perspexero voluntates Nobilium,*
I will write vnto thee.	a. 1. 1. 69.	*scribam ad te.*
I make account the rest wil be sumptuous,	a. 1. 1. 70.	*catera spero prolixa esse,*
at the least amongst these competitors of the City:	a. 1. 1. 71.	*his duntaxat vrbanis competitoribus.*
labour thou for me,	a. 1. 1. 72.	(a.1.1.72.a.) *tu mihi cura,*
that thou get me that helping hand	a. 1. 1. 72.a	*illam manum* (a.1. 1.72.a.) *vt prastes*
(because thou art neerer)	a. 1. 1. 73.	(*quoniam propius abes*)
of our friend *Pompeius,*	a. 1. 1. 74.	Pompeij *nostri amici.*
tell him I will not be angry with him,	a. 1. 1. 75.	*nega me ei iratum fore,*
if he come not to my promotion.	a. 1. 1. 76.	*si ad mea commitia non venerit.*
And	a. 1. 1. 77.	*Atque*
these things goe thus.	a. 1. 1. 78.	*hac huiusmodi sunt.*
But	a. 1. 1. 79.	*Sed*

I must

I muſt earneſtly requeſt you to pardon mee for one thing :	a. 1.	1. 80.	*eſt, quòd abs te mihi ignoſci peruelim.*
Cæcilius	a. 1.	1. 81.	Cæcilius
thine Vncle by the Mother,	a. 1.	1. 82.	*Auunculus tuus,*
being by *Publius Varius* defrauded of a great ſumme of money,	a. 1.	1. 83.	*à* Publ. Vario *cum magna pecunia frauderetur,*
is falne in Law with *Caninius Satyrus,* his brother,	a. 1.	1. 84.	*agere capit cum eius fratre* Caninio Satyro,
about thoſe things,	a. 1.	1. 85.	*de ijs rebus,*
which he ſaid	a. 1.	1. 86.	*quas* (a. 1. 1. 87. a.) *diceret.*
he of purpoſe to deceiue him, had bought of *Varius,*	a. 1.	1. 86. a	*eum dolo malo mancipio accepiſſe de* Vario,
the reſt of the creditors ioyned with him in the ſute.	a. 1.	1. 87.	*vnà agebant cæteri creditores,*
amongſt which	a. 1.	1. 88.	*in quibus*
was *Lucullus,*	a. 1.	1. 89.	*erat Lucullus,*
and	a. 1.	1. 90.	*&*
Publius Scipio,	a. 1.	1. 91.	Pub. Scipio,
and	a. 1.	1. 92.	*&*

Lucius

Lucius Pontius, whom they thought fit to be ouerſeer,	a. 1.	I. 93.	*is quem putabant magiſtrum fore*(a.1.1. 94.a.) L.Pontius,
if the goods were to be ſold,	a. 1.	I. 93. a	*ſi bona venirent,*
but	a. 1.	I. 94.	*verùm*
this is ridiculous	a. 1.	I. 95.	*hoc ridiculum eſt*
to thinke of an o-uerſeer already.	a. 1.	I. 96.	*de magiſtro nunc cognoſcere.*
Cæcilius intreated me	a. 1.	I. 97.	*rogauit me* Cæcili-us,
to appeare [for him] againſt *Satyrus.*	a. 1.	I. 98.	*vt adeſſem contra Satyrum.*
Ther's ſcarſe a day [paſſeth,]	a. 1.	I. 99.	*dies ferè nullus eſt,*
but this *Satyrus* comes often to my houſe.	a. 1.	I.100.	*quin hic* Satyrus *domum meam venti-tet.*
He courts *L. Do-mitius* aboue all o-thers :	a. 1.	I.101.	*obſeruat* L. Domi-tium *maximè,*
[and] hee holds me the next :	a. 1.	I.102.	*me habet proximum :*
he ſtood mee and my brother *Quintus* in great ſteed	a. 1.	I.103.	*fuit & mihi & Qu. fratri magno vſui*
when we ſtood to be Magiſtrates.	a. 1.	I.104.	*in noſtris petitioni-bus.*

Verily

Verily	a. 1.	1.105.	*Sanè*
I am much distur-bed,	a. 1.	1. 106.	*sum perturbatus,*
aswell	a. 1.	1. 107.	*cùm*
for the familiarity of *Satyrus* himselfe,	a. 1.	1.108.	*ipsius* Satyri *fami-liaritate,*
as also	a. 1.	1.109.	*tum*
of *Domitius.*	a. 1.	1. 110.	Domitij,
in whom onely our pretence of ho-nour especially de-pendeth,	a. 1.	1.111.	*in quo vno, maximè ambitio nostra nititur,*
I haue made these [respects] knowne vnto *Cæcilius:*	a. 1.	1.112.	*Demonstraui hæc* Cæcilio :
Shewing him with-all,	a. 1.	1.113.	*Simul & illud o-stendi,*
if he should con-tend with him hand to hand,	a. 1.	1.114.	*si ipse vnus cum illo vno contenderet,*
that I would haue pleasued him.	a. 1.	1.115.	*me ei satisfacturum fuisse.*
[But as the mat-ter] now [stands]	a. 1.	1.116.	*nunc*
in the cause of all the creditors in ge-nerall, especially be-ing men of greatest quality,	a. 1.	1.117.	*in causa vniuerso-rum creditorum, homi-num præsertim amplis-simorum,*

who

who could eafily profecute the common caufe,	a. 1. 1.118.	qui (a.1. 1. 118.a.) facile communem caufam fuftinerent,
without him that Cacilius had entertained in his owne name,	a. 1. 1.118.a	fine eo quem Cæcilius fuo nomine perhiberet,
that it was great reafon,	a. 1. 1.119.	æquum effe,
that he fhould as well confider mine owne occafions, as [the quality of] the time.	a. 1. 1.120.	eum & officio meo confulere,& tempori.
This hee feemes to me to take worfe,	a. 1. 1. 121.	Durius accipere hoc mihi vifus eft,
then I would,	a. 1. 1.122.	quam vellem,
and	a. 1. 1.123.	&
then men of a faire condition are wont:	a. 1. 1.124.	quam homines belli folent :
and	a. 1. 1.125.	&
afterward	a. 1. 1. 126.	poftea
altogether	a. 1. 1.127.	prorfus
he fhunned, what he might, our converfation begun but lately.	a. 1. 1.128.	ab inftituta noftra paucorum dierum confuetudine longè refugit.
I defire you	a. 1. 1.129.	Abs te peto,

that

that you would pardon me herein	a. 1.	1.130.	*vt mihi hoc ignoscas,*
and	a. 1.	1.131.	*&*
[that] you would thinke me	a. 1.	1.132.	*me existimes*
to be prohibited in ciuilitie,	a. 1.	1.133.	*humanitate esse prohibitum,*
to stirre against the especiall reputation of a friend	a. 1.	1.134.	*ne contra amici summam existimátionem* (a. 1. 1. 134.a.) *venirem,*
in his greatest extremitie,	a. 1.	1.134. a	*miserrimo eius tempore,*
he hauing done all his endeauor and good offices for me.	a. 1.	1.135.	*cum is omnia sua studia, & officia in me contulisset.*
But if thou wilt make the worst construction of it,	a. 1.	1.136.	*Quod si voles in me esse durior,*
thou wilt thinke my ambition would not suffer me.	a. 1.	1.137.	*ambitionem mihi putabis obstitisse.*
But	a. 1. 1.138.		(a.1.1.138.a) *Autem*
I am of opinion,	a. 1. 1.138. a		*ego* (a.1.1.138.) *arbitror,*
though that bee the matter	a. 1.	1.139.	*etiamsi id sit*

that

that I am to bee pardoned :	a. 1. 1.140.	*mihi ignoscendum esse :*	
for I feek no greater honour then befeemeth me.	a. 1. 1.141.	ἐπεὶ ὁκ ἰσχύεον ὑδὲ βούλω.	quoniam ne-que victi-mam neque pellem boui-nam [expe-to]
For thou feeft	a. 1. 1.142.	*vides enim*	
in what courfe we are,	a. 1. 1.143.	*in quo curfu fumus,*	[Forte] fi-mus.
and	a. 1. 1.144.	*&*	
how [neceffarie] we thinke it, that all fauours fhould not onely be kept, but alfo fought.	a. 1. 1.145.	*quàm omnes gratias non modo retinēdas, verùm etiam acquirendas putemus.*	
I hope	a. 1. 1.146.	*fpero*	
[that] I haue iuftified my caufe vnto you.	a. 1. 1.147.	*tibi me caufam probàffe.*	Me tibi
Indeed I defire it fhould be fo.	a. 1. 1.148.	*Cupio quidem certè.*	
Thy Statua of *Mercury* and *Minerua* delights me much,	a. 1. 1.149.	Hermathena *tua valdè me delectat,*	
and	a. 1. 1.150.	*&*	
it is fo well placed,	a. 1. 1.151.	*pofita ita bellè eft,*	
that the whole Academy feemes to be the Suns Palace.	a. 1. 1.152.	*vt totum gymnafium ἰνιχ ἀνάσηψα effe videatur.*	Solis bafilica.

Wee

Wee loue thee well.	a. 1.	1.153.	*Multùm te amamus.*	
Lucius Iulius Cæsar, and *Caius Martius Figulus* being Consuls,	a. 1.	1.154.	L. Iulio Cælare, C. Martio Figulo *Coss.*	
Know that I haue a little sonne more then I had,	a. 1.	1.155.	*Filiolo me auctum scito,*	
Terentia being safely deliuered.	a. 1.	1. 156.	*Saluâ* Terentia.	
Not a letter from you all this while?	a. 1.	2. 1.	*Abs te tam diu nihil literarum?*	
I haue formerly written to you of mine owne occasions diligently.	a. 1.	2. 2.	*Ego de meis ad te rationibus scripsi antea diligenter.*	
At this present	a. 1.	2. 3.	*Hoc tempore*	
we make account to defend *Cataline* our Competitor.	a. 1.	2. 4.	*Catilinam, competitorem nostrum, defendere cogitamus.*	
We haue the Iudges we desired,	a. 1.	2. 5.	*Iudices habemus quos voluimus,*	
with the speciall good liking of the Plaintife.	a. 1.	2. 6.	*summâ accusatoris voluntate.*	
I hope,	a. 1.	2. 7.	*Spero,*	
if he shall bee absolued or quit,	a. 1.	2. 8.	*si absolutus erit,*	

he will fticke clo-fer vnto vs	a. 1.	2.	9.	*coniunctiorem nobis fore*
in the occafion of our petition :	a. 1.	2.	10.	*in ratione petitionis :*
but if it fall out o-therwife,	a. 1.	2.	11.	*fin aliter acciderit,*
wee will beare .t patiently.	a. 1.	2.	12.	*humaniter feremus.*
Wee haue neede of your comming betimes.	a. 1.	2.	13.	*Tuo aduentu nobis opus eft maturo.*
For	a. 1.	2.	14.	*Nam*
altogether	a. 1.	2.	15.	*prorfus*
men are of an af-fured opinion,	a. 1.	2.	16.	*fumma hominum eft opinio,*
that thy familiars, Nobly defcended, will bee aduerfaries to our honour.	a. 1.	2.	17.	*tuos familiares, No-biles homines, aduerfa-rios honori noftro fore.*
To reconcile them to me,	a. 1.	2.	18.	*Ad eorum volunta-tem mihi cöciliandam,*
I find you will be of greateft vfe vnto me.	a. 1.	2.	19.	*maximo te mihi v-fui fore video.*
Wherefore,	a. 1.	2.	20.	*Quare*
at the beginning of Ianuarie,	a. 1.	2.	21.	*Ianuario ineunte,*

as

as you haue appointed,	a. 1.	2. 22.	*vt conſtituiſti,*
be ſure	a. 1.	2. 23.	*cura,*
that you bee at Rome.	a. 1.	2. 24.	*vt Romæ ſis.*
Know,	a. 1.	2. 25.	(a.1.2. 25.a.) *Scito,*
thy Grandmother is dead,	a. 1.	2. 25.a	*Auiam tuam* (a.1. 2.25.) *mortuam eſſe,*
out of a deſire to ſee thee,	a. 1.	2. 25.b	*deſiderio tui,*
and withall,	a. 1.	2. 26.	*& ſimul,*
becauſe ſhee feared,	a. 1.	2. 27.	*quòd verita ſit,*
leſt the Latines ſhould not continue their wonted office,	a. 1.	2. 28.	*nè Latinæ in officio non manerent,*
and	a. 1.	2. 29.	*&*
ſhould not bring the ſacrifices into Mount-Alban.	a. 1.	2. 30.	*in montem Albanum hoſtias non adducerent.*
I thinke	a. 1.	2. 31.	(a.1.2.31.b.a.)*Arbitror.*
Lucius Sauſeius will ſend ſome comfortable meſſage	a. 1.	2. 31.a	*conſolationem* (a.1. 2.31.c.) Lu. Sauſeium miſſurum eſſe
of this	a. 1.	2. 31.b	*eius rei*
vnto thee.	a. 1.	2. 31.c	*ad te.*

We

We looke for you here in Ianuary ;	a. 1.	2.	32.	*Nos hîc te ad men-sem Ianuarium expe-ctamus ;*
comes it from re-port,	a. 1.	2.	33.	*ex quodam rumore,*
or	a. 1.	2.	34.	*an*
from your letters sent to others ?	a. 1.	2.	35.	*ex literis tuis ad ali-os mißis ?*
Thou wrot'ſt no-thing	a. 1.	2.	36.	*(a.1.2.36.a.b.) ni-hil ſcripſiſti*
to me	a. 1.	2.	36. a	ad me
thereof.	a. 1.	2.	36. b	*de eo.*
The Statua's are disbarqued at Caie-ta,	a. 1.	2.	37.	*Signa (a.1.2.37.a) ea ſunt ad Caietam ex-poſita.*
which thou pro-curedſt me.	a. 1.	2.	37. a	*quæ nobis curaſti,*
Wee haue not ſeene them,	a. 1.	2.	38.	*Nos ea non vidi-mus,*
neither had we a-ny oportunity to get out of Rome,	a. 1.	2.	39.	*Neque enim exeun-di Roma poteſtas nobis fuit,*
wee haue ſent one to pay for the fraught of them.	a. 1.	2.	40.	*miſimus qui pro vectura ſolueret.*
We loue you ve-ry well,	a. 1.	2.	41.	*Te multùm ama-mus,*
that	a. 1.	2.	42.	*quòd*

thou

thou haſt with diligence procured them, and for a ſmall matter.	a. 1. 2. 43.	*ea abs te diligenter paruóque curata ſunt.*
That which you haue often written vnto me,	a. 1. 2. 44.	*Quod ad me ſæpè ſcripſiſti,*
about the pacifying of our friend,	a. 1. 2. 45.	*de noſtro amico placando,*
I haue effected,	a. 1. 2. 46.	*feci,*
and	a. 1. 2. 47.	*&*
I haue tryed all things.	a. 1. 2. 48.	*expertus ſum omnia.*
But	a. 1. 2. 49.	*Sed*
his mind is marueilouſly alienated:	a. 1. 2. 50.	*mirandum in modum eſt animo abalienati:*
vpon what ſuſpitions,	a. 1. 2. 51.	*auibus de ſuſpitionibus,*
although	a. 1. 2. 52.	*etſi*
I make account that you haue heard;	a. 1. 2. 53.	*audiſſe te arbitror;*
yet	a. 1. 2. 54.	*tamen*
when you come,	a. 1. 2. 55.	*(a. 1. 2. 25. a.) cùm veneris,*
you ſhall know of me.	a. 1. 2. 55. a	*ex me (a. 1. 2. 55.) cognoſces.*

Y

I could not	a. 1. 2. 56.	(a.1.2.56.a.b.)*Non potui*
reftore *Saluftius* [who is] prefent,	a. 1. 2. 56.a	Saluftium *prafentem reftituere*
to his ancient fauour.	a. 1. 2. 56.b	*in eius veterem gratiam.*
I haue hereupon written this vnto thee,	a. 1. 2. 57.	*Hoc eò ad te fcripfi,*
becaufe	a. 1. 2. 58.	*quòd*
he was woont to accufe mee about thee :	a. 1. 2. 59.	*is me accufare de te folebat :*
he made triall in himfelfe	a. 1. 2. 60.	*in fe expertus eft*
that he is harder to be intreated,	a. 1. 2. 61.	*illum effe minùs exorabilem,*
[and] that I haue not beene behindhand with thee in what I was able.	a. 1. 2. 62.	*meum ftudium nec tibi defuiffe.*
Wee haue betrothed little *Tullia* to *Caius Pifo Frugi,* fon of *Lucius.*	a. 1. 2. 63.	Tulliolam C.Pifoni, L. f. Frugi,*defpondimus.* *C.Caio L.Lucij f. filio.*
Farewell.	a. 1. 2. 64.	*Vale.*
Thou makeft vs often to expect thee.	a.1. 3. 1.	*Crebras expectationes nobis tui cõmoues.*
And of late	a. 1. 3. 2.	*Nuper quidem*

when

when we thought thou waſt come neere vs,	a. **1.** 3.	3.	*cùm iam te aduenta-re arbitraremur,*
on the ſudden	a. **1.** 3.	4.	*repentè*
thou haſt put vs off till Iuly.	a. **1.** 3.	5.	*abs te in mēſem Quin-tilem reiecti ſumus.*
But now	a. **1.** 3.	6.	*Nunc verò*
I hold it beſt	a. **1.** 3.	7.	*ſentio*
(if thou canſt)	a. **1.** 3.	8.	*(quod commodo tuo facere poteris)*
that thou ſhould'ſt come	a. **1.** 3.	9.	*venias*
at that time	a. **1.** 3.	10.	*ad id tempus*
thou haſt deter-mined in thy letters,	a. **1.** 3.	11.	*quod ſcribis,*
thou wilt come iuſt to the prefer-ment of my brother Quintus:	a. **1.** 3.	12.	*obieris* Quinti *fra-tris commitia :*
after a long while thou wilt come to ſee vs :	a. **1.** 3.	13.	*nos longo interuallo viſeris :*
thou wilt end the controuerſie be-tweene thee and A-cutilius.	a. **1.** 3.	14.	Acutilianam *con-trouerſiam tranſegeris.*
And Peducæus bid me write thus much vnto thee :	a. **1.** 3.	15.	*Hoc me etiam* Pe-ducæus *vt ad te ſcri-berem admonuit :*

for

For wee thinke it profitable	a. 1.	3.	16.	*putamus enim vtile esse*
that thou should'ſt now at length come to an agreement about the buſineſſe.	a. 1.	3.	17.	*te aliquando iam rem tranſigere.*
I am and haue bin alwaies ready to arbitrate betweene you.	a. 1.	3.	18.	*Mea interceſſio & eſt & fuit parata.*
Wee haue heere determined the buſineſſe of *Caius Macer*,	a.1.	3.	19.	*Nos hîc* (a.1.3.19. a.)*de* C.Macro *tranſegimus,*
with incredible and ſingular liking of the people,	a. 1.	3.	19.a	*incredibli, ac ſingulari populi voluntate,*
to whom though we haue been iuſt,	a. 1.	3.	20.	*cui cùm æqui fuiſſemus,*
yet	a. 1.	3.	21.	*tamen*
we haue receiued much greater benefit,	a. 1.	3.	22.	*multò maiorem fructum* (a.1.3.22.a.b.) *cepimus,*
from the eſteeme of the people	a. 1.	3.	22.a	*ex populi exiſtimatione*
by his condemnation,	a. 1.	3.	22.b	*illo condemnato,*

then

then wee had re-ceiued from his fauour,	a. 1.	3. 23.	quàm ex ipsius, (a. 1.3. 23.a.) gratia cepissemus.
if hee had been quit.	a. 1.	3. 23.a	si absolutus esset.
Concerning that which thou wroteft vnto me	a. 1.	3. 24.	Quod ad me (a.3. 24.a.) scribis,
about the Statua of Mercurie and Minerua,	a. 1.	3. 24.a	de Hermathena,
it is an ornament proper vnto mine owne Academie, very gratefull to me,	a. 1.	3. 25.	per mihi gratnm est ornamentum Academiæ proprium meæ,
in that	a. 1.	3. 26.	quòd
both	a. 1.	3. 27.	&
Hermes belongs to all,	a. 1.	3. 28.	Hermes commune omnium
and	a. 1.	3. 29.	&
Minerua belongs particularly to that place of exercise.	a. 1.	3. 30.	Minerua singulare est eius Gymnasij.
Wherefore	a. 1.	3. 31.	Quare
I would	a. 1.	3. 32.	velim
as thou writeft	a. 1.	3. 33.	vt scribis

that

that thou would'ft alfo adorne that place with many other things.	a. 1.	3. 34.	*cæteris quoque rebus quamplurimis eum locum ornes.*
The Statua's thou fent'ft mee heretofore,	a. 1.	3. 35.	*Quæ mihi antea figna mififti,*
I haue not yet feene :	a. 1.	3. 36.	*ea nondum vidi :*
they are in Formianum :	a. 1.	3. 37.	*in Formiano funt :*
whither I at this prefent thought to goe.	a. 1.	3. 38.	*quò ego nunc proficifci cogitabam.*
I will carry all of them into Tufculanum.	a. 1.	3. 39.	*Illa omnia in Tufculanum deportabo.*
If I euer grow to be richer,	a. 1.	3. 40.	(a. 1. 3. 40. a.) *Si quando abundare capero,*
I will garnifh Caieta.	a. 1.	3. 40. a	*Caietam* (a. 1. 3. 40. a.) *ornabo.*
Keepe thy books,	a. 1.	3. 41.	*libros tuos conferua,*
and	a. 1.	3. 42.	*&*
bee not out of hope,	a. 1.	3. 43.	*noli defperare,*
that I may make them mine :	a. 1.	3. 44.	*eos meos facere poffe ;*

Eos me meos facere.

which

which if I com-paſſe,	a. 1.	3.	45.		*quod ſi aſſequor,*
I am richer then *Craſſus,*	a. 1.	3.	46.		*ſupero* Craſſum *di-uitijs,*
and	a. 1.	3.	47.		*atque*
I deſpiſe all mens Villages and Med-dowes.	a. 1.	3.	48.		*omnium vicos & prata contemno.*
Farewell.	a. 1.	3.	49.		*Vale.*
How much griefe I haue taken,	a. 1.	4.	1.		*Quantum dolorem acceperim,*
and	a. 1.	4.	2.		*&*
of how much fruit I am depriued	a. 1.	4.	3.		*quanto fructu ſim priuatus*
as well in matter of Iuſtice, as dome-ſtick affaires,	a. 1.	4.	4.		*& forenſi, & dome-ſtico,*
through the death of our brother *Luci-us,*	a. 1.	4.	5.		*L. fratris noſtri mor-te,*
eſpecially	a. 1.	4.	6.		*inprimis*
for our conuerſa-tion,	a. 1.	4.	7.		*pro noſtra conſuetu-dine,*
thou mayſt con-iecture.	a. 1.	4.	8.		*tu exiſtimare potes.*
For	a. 1.	4.	9.		*Nam*
from him I had all things,	a. 1.	4.	10.		*mihi omnia* (a. 1.4. 10.a.)*ex illo accidebāt.*

which

which can as delightfull happen to any man,	a. 1.	4.	10.a	*quæ iucunda* (a. 1. 4.10.b.) *homini accidere poſſunt,*
out of another mans courteſie and carriage:	a. 1.	4.	10.b	*ex humanitate alterius & moribus :*
Wherefore	a. 1.	4.	11.	*Quare*
I doubt not,	a. 1.	4.	12.	*non dubito,*
but it is alſo a trouble to thee,	a. 1.	4.	13.	*quin tibi quoque id moleſtum ſit,*
ſeeing	a. 1.	4.	14.	*cùm*
thou wilt both be moued with my griefe,	a. 1.	4.	15.	*& meo dolore moueare,*
and	a. 1.	4.	16.	*&*
thou thy ſelf ſhalt loſe one of thine alliance, and a friend,	a. 1.	4.	17.	*ipſe* (a.1.4.17.a.b.) *affinem, amicúmque amiſeris,*
exceedingly adorned with all vertue and officiouſneſſe,	a. 1.	4.	17.a	*omni virtute officióque ornatiſſimum,*
and one that loued thee,	a. 1.	4.	17.b	*tuíque* (a. 1. 4.17. c.d.e.f. *amantem,*
as well	a. 1.	4.	17.c	*&*
of his owne accord,	a. 1.	4.	17.d	*ſua ſponte,*
as	a. 1.	4.	17.e	*&*
vpon my ſpeech.	a. 1.	4.	17.f	*meo ſermone.*

About

About that you write vnto me	a.	1.	4.	18.	*Quod ad me scribis*
concerning your sister,	a.	1.	4.	19.	*de sorore tua,*
shee shall testifie vnto you,	a.	1.	4.	20.	*testis erit tibi ipsa,*
what care I tooke of her,	a.	1.	4.	21.	*quantæ mihi curæ fuerit,*
that the mind of my brother *Quintus* might be such vnto her,	a.	1.	4.	22.	*vt Qu. fratris animus in eam esset is,*
as it ought:	a.	1.	4.	23.	*qui esse deberet :*
thinking him to be otherwise bent then he should,	a.	1.	4.	24.	*quem cùm esse offensiorem arbitrarer,*
I wrote such letters vnto him,	a.	1.	4.	25.	*eas literas ad eum misi,*
whereby	a.	1.	4.	26.	*quibus,*
I might appease him as a brother,	a.	1.	4.	27.	*& placarem vt fratrem,*
and	a.	1.	4.	28.	*&*
aduise him as my Iunior,	a.	1.	4.	29.	*monerem vt minorem,*
and	a.	1.	4.	30.	*&*
reprehend him, as in an error.	a.	1.	4.	31.	*obiurgarem, vt errantem.*
Therefore	a.	1.	4.	32.	*Itaque*
by those [letters]	a.	1.	4.	33.	*ex ijs*

which

which afterwards he often wrote vnto me,	a. 1.	4. 34.	quæ poſteà ſæpè ab eo ad me ſcripta ſunt,
I truſt	a. 1.	4. 35.	confido
that all things ſtand ſo	a. 1.	4. 36.	ita eſſe omnia
as they ſhould, and we would.	1. 1.	4. 37.	vt & oporteat, & velimus.
About the ſending of letters,	a. 1.	4. 38.	De literarum miſſione,
I am accuſed by thee	a. 1.	4. 39.	(a. 1.4.39.a.) abs te accuſor
without cauſe:	a. 1.	4. 39.a	ſine cauſa :
for I neuer was certified,	a. 1.	4. 40.	nunquam enim (a. 1.4.40.a.) certior ſum factus,
frō our Pomponia,	a. 1.	4. 40. a	à Pomponia noſtra,
that there was any meſſenger.	a. 1.	4. 41.	eſſe cui literas dare poſſem.
And further,	a. 1.	4. 42.	Porrò autem,
I neither had the oportunitie,	a. 1.	4. 43.	neque mihi accidit,
to haue,	a. 1.	4. 44.	vt haberem,
any man that went into Epirus.	a. 1.	4. 45.	qui in Epirum proficiſceretur.
Nor as yet	a.1.	4. 46.	Neque-dum
did we heare thou waſt at Athens.	a. 1.	4. 47.	te Athenis eſſe audiebamus.

But

But touching the caufe of _Acutilius_,	a. 1. 4. 48.	_De_ Acutiliano _autem negotio_,
I had done what you commanded.	a. 1. 4. 49.	_quod mihi mandà-ras_ (a. 1. 4.49.a.)_con-feceram :_
Affoone as I came to Rome	a. 1. 4. 49.a	_vt primum_ (a. 1.4. 49.b.) _Romam veni_
after your depar-ture,	a. 1.4. 49.b	_à tuo digreſſu,_
but	a. 1. 4. 50.	_ſed_
it fell out,	a. 1. 4. 51.	_accidit,_
that both conten-tion was needleffe,	a. 1. 4. 52.	_vt & contentione nihil opus eſſet,_
and	a. 1. 4. 53.	_&_
I,	a. 1. 4. 54.	_ego,_
who haue thought thee fufficiently able to counfell thy felfe.	a. 1. 4. 55.	_qui in te ſatis conſi-lij ſtatuerim eſſe,_
I had rather _Pedu-cæus_ fhuld giue thee counfell by letters, then my felfe.	a. 1. 4. 56.	_Mallem_ Peducæ-um _tibi conſilium per literas, quàm me dare._
For	a. 1. 4. 57.	_Etenim_
I hauing for ma-ny dayes harkned to _Acutilius,_	a. 1. 4. 58.	_cùm multos dies au-res meas_ Acutilio _de-diſſem,_
whofe manner of fpeech, I fuppofe you know,	a. 1. 4. 59.	_cuius ſermonis genus, tibi notum eſſe arbi-tror,_

I

I haue not thought it troublesome to me	a. 1.	4.	60.	*non mihi graue duxi*
to write vnto thee	a. 1.	4.	61.	*scribere ad te*
of his complaints,	a. 1.	4.	62.	*de illius querimonijs,*
I hauing reputed the hearing of them no trouble.	a. 1.	4.	63.	*cùm eas audire (a. 1. 4.59.a.) leue putâssem.*
(which was some-what noysome)	a. 1.	4.	63.a	*(quod erat subodiosum)*
But	a. 1.	4.	64.	*Sed*
from thy selfe	a. 1.	4.	65.	*abs te ipso*
who accusest me,	a. 1.	4.	66.	*qui me accusas,*
know there is but one letter come vn-to me,	a. 1.	4.	67.	*vnas mihi scito lite-ras redditas esse,*
though thou hast both more leasure to write, and better meanes of sending.	a. 1.	4.	68.	*cùm & otij ad scri-bendum plus, & facul-tatem dandi maiorem habueris.*
Whereas thou wri-test,	a. 1.	4.	69.	*Quod scribis,*
that I ought to reconcile any man vnto thee, that were set against thee,	a. 1.	4.	70.	*etiam si cuius ani-mus in te esset offensior, à me recolligi oportere,*
I conceiue thee.	a. 1.	4.	71.	*quid dicas ?*
neither haue I neg-lected it :	a. 1.	4.	72.	*neque id neglexi :*

Sc.scio,&c.

But

But	a. 1.	4. 73.	*Sed*
he is wondroufly troubled,	a. 1.	4. 74.	*eſt miro quodam modo affectus,*
and I haue not omitted [thoſe things]	a. 1.	4. 75.	*Ego autem (a. 1. 4. 75.a.b.) non præterÿ.*
which were to be ſpoken	a. 1.	4. 75.a	*quæ dicenda fuerunt*
about thee.	a. 1.	4. 75.b	*de te.*
But what ſhould be attempted,	a. 1.	4. 76.	*Quid autem contendendum eſſet,*
I thought fit to be determined according to your owne pleaſure :	a. 1.	4. 77.	*ex tua putabam voluntate ſtatuere oportere :*
which if you ſhall write vnto me,	a. 1.	4. 78.	*quam ſi ad me perſcripſeris,*
you ſhall vnderſtand,	a. 1.	4. 79.	*intelliges,*
that I would neither haue been more diligent,	a. 1.	4. 80.	*me neque diligentiorem eſſe voluiſſe,*
then thou wouldeſt haue been,	a. 1.	4. 81.	*quàm tu eſſes,*
nor haue beene hereafter more negligent,	a. 1.	4. 82.	*neque negligentiorem fore,*
then you would haue me.	a. 1.	4. 83.	*quàm tu velis.*

Of the Tadian bufineffe,	a. 1. 4. 84.	De Tadiana re,
Tadius hath told me,	a. 1. 4. 85.	mecum Tadius locutus eft,
that thou haft written in this manner,	a. 1. 4. 86.	te ita fcripfiffe,
that now there was no need that he fhould take any farther care,	a. 1. 4. 87.	nihil effe iam quod laboraret,
becaufe the inheritance fhould be attained by prefcription.	a. 1. 4. 88.	quoniam hæreditas vfucapta effet.
Wee marueiled that you were ignorant of this,	a. 1. 4. 89.	Id mirabamur, te ignorare,
of the lawfull guardianfhip,	a. 1. 4. 90.	de tutela legitima,
wherein	a. 1. 4. 91.	in qua
the Maide is reported to be,	a. 1. 4. 92.	dicitur effe puella,
that nothing can be attained by prefcription.	a. 1. 4. 93.	nihil vfucapi poffe.
I am glad	a. 1. 4. 94.	(a.1.4.94.a.)Gaudeo
the Epirotick purchafe pleafeth you.	a. 1. 4. 94 .a	Epiroticam emptionem (a.1.4.94.a.) tibi placere.

The

The things which I haue committed vnto thee,	a. 1. 4. 95.	*Quæ tibi mandaui,*
and	a. 1. 4. 96.	*&*
thofe which thou fhalt thinke fitting for our *Tufculanum,*	a. 1. 4. 97.	*quæ tu intelliges conuenire noftro* Tufculano,
I would haue thee be carefull of,	a. 1. 4. 98.	*velim* (a.1.4.98.a.) *cures,*
as thou writeft [thou wilt be,]	a. 1. 4. 98.a	*vt fcribis,*
fo farre forth as thou canft,	a. 1. 4. 99.	*quod* (a.1.4. 99. a.) *facere poteris,*
without thine owne preiudice.	a. 1. 4. 99.a	*fine moleftia tua.*
For	a. 1. 4.100.	*Nam*
Wee are onely in that place at quiet from al troubles and bufineffe,	a. 1. 4.101.	*nos ex omnibus moleftijs & laboribus vno illo in loco conquiefcimus :*
where wee daily looke for my brother.	a. 1. 4.102.	*quo fratrem quotidiè expectamus.*
Terentia hath great paines of the ioynts,	a. 1. 4.103.	Terentia *magnos articulorū dolores habet,*
and	a. 1. 4.104.	*&*

fhee

fhee loues thee, thy fifter and mother exceedingly :	a. 1.	4.105.	te, fororémque tuam & matrem maximè diligit :
and fhe with little *Tullia* our darling, falutes thee heartily.	a. 1.	4.106.	falutémque tibi plurimam adfcribit, & Tulliola *deliciæ noftræ.*
Be carefull,	a. 1.	4.107.	*cura,*
to keepe thine owne health, and to loue vs :	a. 1.	4.108.	*vt valeas, & nos ames :*
and	a. 1.	4.109.	*&*
perfwade thy felfe,	a. 1	4.110.	*tibi perfuadeas,*
that I loue thee as a brother.	a. 1.	4 111.	*te à me fraternè amari.*
Farewell.	a. 1.	4.112.	*Vale.*
I will do nothing	a. 1.	5. 1.	*Non committam*
hereafter	a. 1.	5. 2.	*pofthac*
that you may accufe mee of negligence in writing letters.	a. 1.	5. 3.	*vt me accufare de epiftolarum negligentia pofsis.*
Looke you now to it,	a 1.	5. 4.	*Tu modò videto,*
liuing in fo great leifure,	a. 1.	5. 5.	*in tanto otio,*
that you equalize me.	a. 1.	5. 6.	*vt par mihi fis.*

Marcus

Marcus Fonteius Pontius hath at Naples bought the Rabirian houſe for an hundred and thirtie thouſand Seſtertij,	a. 1. 5. 7.	*Domum Rabirianam Neapoli* (a. 1. 5. 8.) *M. Font. Pont. emit* H̶S̶.ccci⊃⊃xxx.	Seſtertijs centum triginta millibus.
which you had in conceit already meaſured and new built.	a. 1. 5. 8,	*quam tu iam dimenſam, & adificatam animo habebas.*	
This I deſired you ſhould know,	a. 1. 5. 9.	*Id te ſcire volui,*	
if peraduenture it might concerne you any thing.	a. 1. 5. 10.	*ſi quid fortè ea res ad cogitationes tuas pertineret.*	
My brother *Quintus* beares the ſame mind towards *Pomponia* that we would haue him,	a. 1. 5. 11.	*Q. frater* (a. 1. 5. 11.) *quo volumus animo eſt in* Pomponiam,	
as farre as I can perceiue,	a. 1. 5. 12.	*(vt mihi videtur)*	
and	a. 1. 5. 13.	*&*	
he was now with her at the Manor of Arpinas,	a. 1. 5. 14.	*cum ea nunc in Arpinati pradio erat,*	Nunc eram.
he had with him *Decimus Turranius*, a nimble and expert man.	a. 1. 5. 15.	*ſecum habebat hominem* χϱηϲιμώϑη, Decimum Turranium.	Nauum, & qui vſu occalluit.

Our

Our Father de-parted from vs	a. 1.	5.	16.	*Pater nobis deceßit,*
on the eighth of the Kalends of December.	a. 1.	5.	17.	*ad* VIII. *Kalendas* Octauum *Decembres.*
This was almost all	a. 1.	5.	18.	*hæc habebam ferè*
I had to say vnto you.	a. 1.	5.	19.	*quæ te scire vellem.*
I would not haue you ouerslip [the occasion,]	a. 1.	5.	20.	*Tu velim* (a. 1. 5. 20. a. b. c.) *ne præter-mittas,*
if thou canst find any ornaments that are proper for the Academie,	a. 1.	5.	20.a	*si qua ornamenta* γυμνασιώδη *reperire pote-ris,* Gymnasio præcipuè conuenien-tia.
which may be-come that place	a. 1.	5.	20.b	*quæ loci sint eius,*
which thou wot-test of.	a. 1.	5.	20.c	*quem tu non igno-ras.*
We are so delight-ed with Tuscula-num,	a. 1.	5.	21.	*Nos Tusculano ita delectamur,*
that wee please our selues,	a. 1.	5.	22.	*vt nobismet-ipsis* (a. 1. 5. 22. a. b.) *placea-mus.*
then at length,	a. 1.	5.	22.a	*tum denique,*
when wee come thither.	a. 1.	5.	22.b	*cùm illo venimus.*

What

What thou dooſt about all matters,	a. 1. 5. 23.	*Quid agas omnibus de rebus,*
and	a. 1. 5. 24.	*&*
what thou purpo-ſeſt to doe,	a. 1. 5. 25.	*quid acturus ſis,*
let vs bee with all diligence certified.	a. 1. 5. 26.	*fac nos quàm dili-gentiſſimè certiores.*
All goes well with [your] mo-ther :	a. 1. 5. 27.	*Apud matrem re-ctè eſt :*
and wee haue a care of her.	a. 1. 5. 28.	*eáque nobis curæ eſt.*
I haue a purpoſe	a. 1. 5. 29.	*(a. 1. 5. 30. a.) con-ſtitui*
that twenty thou-ſand foure hundred Seſtertij bee procu-red for *Lucius Cin-cius,*	a. 1. 5. 29. a	L. Cincio HS, XXCD. (a. 1. 5. 30.) *me curaturum,*
on the Ides of Fe-bruarie.	a. 1. 5. 30.	*idibus Februarij.*
I would haue you vſe your beſt endea-uour,	a. 1. 5. 31.	*Tu, velim* (a. 1. 5. 30. a.)*des operam.*
that we may haue thoſe things out of hand ;	a. 1. 5. 31. a	*ea,* (a. 1. 5. 30. b.) *vt quam primum ha-beamus ;*

Seſtertiorum viginti milli quadringen-ta.

which

which thou wri-teſt, thou haſt boght and prepared for vs.	a. 1.	5.	31.b	quæ nobis emiſſe & paràſſe ſcribis. (a.1.5. 31.)
and	a. 1.	5.	31.c	&
I would haue you bethinke your ſelfe,	a. 1.	5.	31.d	velim cogites
as you haue pro-miſed me,	a. 1.	5.	31.e	(id quod mihi polli-citus es)
how	a. 1.	5.	31.f	quemadmodum
you may help vs to make vp our library.	a. 1.	5.	31.g	Bybliothecam nobis conficere poſſis.
In thy courteſie wee haue placed all hope of our delight,	a.1	5.	32.	Omnem ſpem delecta-tionis noſtræ(a.1.5.32. a.) in tua humanitate poſitam habemus,
which we meane to haue,	a. 1.	5.	32.a	quam (a.1.5.32.b.) habere volumus,
when wee come to be at leiſure.	a. 1.	5.	32.b	cùm in otium vene-rimus.
Farewell.	a. 1.	5.	33.	Vale.
Thy mother is with thee,	a. 1.	6.	1.	Apud te eſt (a.1. 6.1.a.) mater tua,
as we deſire,	a. 1.	6.	1.a	vt volumus,
and	a.1.	6.	2.	&
your ſiſter is belo-ued of mee, and my brother Quintus.		6.	3.	ſoror à me Quintó-que fratre diligitur.
I haue ſpoken with Acutilius.	a. 1.	6.	4.	Cum Acutilio ſum locutus.

Hee

Hee denies that a-ny thing hath been written to him	a. 1.	6.	5.	*Is sibi negat* (a.1.6. 5.a.) *quidquam scrip-tum esse*
from his Procura-tor;	a. 1.	6.	5. a	*à suo Procuratore;*
and	a. 1.	6.	6.	*&*
he wondreth	a. 1.	6.	7.	*miratur*
that this contro-uersie hath been,	a. 1.	6.	8.	*istam controuersiam fuisse,*
becaufe hee had refufed,	a. 1.	6.	9.	*quòd ille recusárat,*
that you fought no further for fecuritie.	a. 1.	6.	10.	*fatisdari amplius abs te non peti.*
Whereas you write,	a. 1.	6.	11.	*Quod* (a.1.6.11.a.) *fcribis,*
that you haue left the Tadian bufines;	a. 1.	6.	11.a	*te de Tadiano nego-tio decidisse;*
I vnderftand the fame was both ac-ceptable and excee-ding pleafing to *Ta-dius.*	a. 1.	6.	12.	*id ego* Tadio *& gratum esse intellexi, & magnopere iucundum.*
That friend of ours is angry with you,	a. 1.	6.	13.	*Ille noster amicus* (a. 1.6. 13.a.b.c.d.e. f.) *tibi iratus est,*
and	a. 1.	6.	13.a	*&*
indeed	a. 1.	6.	13.b	*mehercule*
an exceeding good man,	a. 1.	6.	13.c	*vir optimus,*

and

and	a. 1. 6. 13.d	*&*
moſt louing to me	a. 1. 6. 13.e	*mihi amiciſſimus*
verily.	a. 1. 6. 13.f	*ſanè.*
When I know what account you make hereof,	a. 1. 6. 14.	*Hoc ſi, quanti tu æ-ſtimes, ſciam,*
then I ſhall know	a. 1. 6. 15.	*tum* (a.1.6.15.a.) *ſcire poſsim,*
what I am to goe vpon.	a. 1. 6. 15. a	*quid mihi elaboran-dum ſit.*
I haue procured twentie thouſand foure hundred Se-ſtertij for *L. Cincius*,	a. 1. 6. 16.	*L. Cincio* HS ccɔɔ·ccɪ ɔɔ·cccc. (a. 1.6.17.a.b.) *curaui.*
for theStatua's that came from Megara,	a.1. 6. 16. a	*pro ſignis Mega-ricis,*
as you wrote vn-to me.	a. 1. 6. 16.b	*vt tu ad me ſcripſe-ras.*
Thy Pentelick Statua's of *Mercury* delight me verie much,	a. 1. 6. 17.	*Hermæ tui Penteli-ci* (a.1.6.17.a.b. c.) *me admodum delcctant,*
with the brazen heads,	a. 1. 6. 17.a	*cum capitibus æneis,*
about which you wrote vnto me	a. 1.6. 17.b	*de quibus ad me ſcripſiſti*
at this inſtant.	a. 1.6. 17. c	*iam nunc.*
Wherefore	a. 1.6. 18.	*Quare*

Seſtertiorum nummorum viginti millia quadrin-genta.

I

I defire thou wouldeft fend both thofe, and the Statua's, and very many other things	a. 1.	6.	19.	*velim & eos & figna, & cetera* (a.1.6.19. a.) *quamplurima* (a.1. 6.19.f.) *mittas*
which you fhall thinke agreeable to that place	a. 1.	6.	19.a	*quæ tibi eius loci* (a. 1.6.19.b.c. d.e.) *effe videbuntur*
and	a. 1.	6.	19.b	*&*
to our affection	a. 1.	6.	19.c	*noftri ftudÿ,*
and	a. 1.	6.	19.d	*&*
to your eligancy,	a. 1.	6.	19.e	*tuæ elegantiæ,*
and [that] as foone as may be,	a. 1.	6.	19. f	*quamprimúmque*
and	a. 1.	6.	20.	*&*
efpecially	a. 1.	6.	21.	*maximè*
thofe things which you fhall thinke fitting for our Academie,	a. 1.	6.	22.	*quæ tibi gymnafÿ* (a.1.22.a.) *videbuntur effe,*
and for the couered place of exercife.	a. 1.	6.	22.a	*xyftique.*
For	a. 1.	6.	23.	*Nam*
in this kind	a. 1.	6.	24.	*in hoc genere*
we are fo carried away with defire,	a. 1.	6.	25.	*fic ftudio efferimur*
that wee are by thee to be furthered [therein.]	a. 1.	6.2	6.	*vt, abs te adiuuandi* (a.1.6.26.a.) *fimus,*

by

by others to bee almoſt reprehended.	a. 1.	6.	26. a	*ab alijs propè reprehendendi.*
If *Lentulus* his ſhip be not [there]	a. 1.	6.	27.	*Si* Lentuli *nauis non erit*
imbarque them where you pleaſe.	a. 1.	6.	28.	*quò tibi placebit imponito.*
Little *Tullia* our pretie paſtime deſires to haue ſome ſmall token from thee,	a. 1.	6.	29.	Tulliola *deliciolæ noſtræ tuum munuſculum flagitat,*
and	a. 1.	6.	30.	*&*
ſhe calls vpon me,	a.1	6.	31.	*me (. 1.6. 31. a.) appellat*
as [your] ſuretie :	a. 1.	6.	31.a	*vt ſponſorem*
but I haue determined rather to forſweare it,	a. 1.	6.	32.	*mihi autem abiurare certius eſt,*
then to pay it.	a. 1.	6.	33.	*quàm dependere.*
Farewell.	a. 1.	6.	34.	*Vale.*
Your letters are brought vs too too ſeldome,	a. 1.	7.	1.	*Nimiùm rarò nobis abs te literæ afferuntur,*
Seeing you may both much eaſier find out,	a. 1.	7.	2.	*cùm & multò tu facilius reperias,*

men

men that are to come to Rome,	a. I.	7.	3.	q̃ i Romam proficiscan tur,
then I	a. I.	7.	4.	quam ego
[men] that [are to goe] to Athens:	a. I.	7.	5.	qui Athenas :
and	a. I.	7.	6.	&
[feeing] it is a thing of greater certaintie to you,	a. I.	7.	7.	certius tibi fit,
that I am at Rome,	a. I.	7.	8.	me effe Roma,
then to me,	a. I.	7.	9.	quàm mihi,
that thou art at Athens.	a. I.	7.	10.	te Athenis.
Therefore	a. I.	7.	11.	Itáque
in refpect of this my doubt,	a. I.	7.	12.	propter hanc dubitationem meam,
this very letter is fhorter,	a. I.	7.	13.	breuior hac ipfa epiftola eft,
in that,	a. I.	7.	14.	quòd,
I being vncertaine	a. I.	7.	15.	cùm incertus effem,
where thou waft,	a. I.	7.	16.	vbi effes,
I was vnwilling that kind of familiar fpeech of ours fhuld come into the hands of ftrangers.	a. I.	7.	17.	nolebam illum noftrum familiarem fermonem in alienas manus deuenire.

[Cùm]

The

The Megaricke Statua's, & the *Mer-curies* I expect infallibly,	a. 1.	7. 18.	*Signa Megarica* & Hermas(a.1.7.18. a) *vehementer expecto.*
of which you wrote vnto me.	a. 1.	7. 18.a	*de quibus ad me scripsisti,*
Whatsoeuer you shall haue of that kind,	a. 1.	7. 19.	*Quicquid eiusdem generis habebis,*
that you may think worthy our Academie,	a. 1.	7. 20.	*dignum Academia tibi quod videbitur,*
make no difficulty to send it,	a. 1.	7. 21.	*ne dubitaris mittere,*
and	a. 1.	7. 22.	*&*
make no doubt but I will pay for them.	a. 1.	7. 23.	*arca nostra confidito.*
In this kind consists my delight,	a. 1.	7. 24.	*Genus hoc est voluptatis mea,*
these things which may especially befit an Academy,	a. 1.	7. 25.	*qua γυμνασιωδη maximè sunt,*
those I seeke after.	a. 1.	. 26.	*ea quaro.*
Lentulus doth promise his shipping.	a. 1.	7. 27.	Lentulus *naues suas pollicetur.*
I request you	a. 1.	7. 28.	*Peto abs te*
to be very carefull of these things,	a. 1.	7. 29.	*vt hac cures diligenter,*

Apta gymnasio.

Chilius

Chilius intreates you,	a. **1.**	7.	30.	Chilius *te rogat,*
and	a. **1.**	7.	31.	*&*
I vpon his requeſt [that you would ſend him] the cuſtomes of the Eumolpidi.	a. **1.**	7.	32.	*ego eius rogatu* Ἐυμολπιδῶν πάτρια.
Farewell.	a. **1.**	7.	33.	*Vale.*
Being in Tuſculanum,	a. **1.**	8.	1.	*Cum eſſem in Tuſculano,*
let this [beginning] bee in exchange for that of yours [where you ſay,]	a. **1.**	8.	2.	*(erit hoc tibi pro illo tuo,*
being in Ceramicum.	a. **1.**	8.	3.	*cum eſſem in Ceramico.)*
But howſoeuer	a. **1.**	8.	4.	*veruntamen*
being there,	a. **1**	8.	5.	*cum ibi eſſem,*
the ſeruant ſent by your ſiſter from Rome, gaue mee a letter that came frō you.	a. **1.**	8.	6.	*Roma puer à ſorore tua miſſus, epiſtolam mihi abs te allatam dedit.*
And he let me vnderſtand,	a. **1.**	8.	7.	*nuntiauitque,*
the ſame day	a. **1.**	8.	8.	*eo ipſo die*
in the afternoone,	a. **1.**	8.	9.	*poſt meridiem,*

Eumolpidarum ritus patrios.

ſhe

fhe was to fend him,	a. 1. 8.	10.	*miffuram eum,*
that fhould goe vnto thee.	a. 1. 8.	11.	*qui ad te proficifce-retur.*
Hence it comes,	a. 1. 8.	12.	*Eò factum eft,*
that I wrote fome-thing in anfwer of your letter,	a. 1. 8.	13.	*vt epiftola tua re-fcriberem aliquid,*
[and that] I was conftrained by the fhortnes of the time to write fo little,	a. 1. 8.	14.	*breuitate temporis tam pauca cogerer fcri-bere.*
Firft,	a. 1. 8.	15.	*Primùm,*
I promife thee,	a. 1. 8.	16.	*tibi (a. 1.8. 16.a.) polliceor,*
about the appea-fing of our friend, or rather about the ful! reftoring him [vnto thee,]	a. 1. 8.	16.a	*de noftro amico pla-cando, aut etiam planè reftituendo.*
Which though formerly I haue of mine owne accord endeauoured;	a. 1. 8.	17.	*Quòd ego etfi meâ fponte antè faciebam,*
yet at this prefent	a. 1. 8.	18.	*eò nunc tamen,*
I will both doe it more induftrioufly,	a. 1. 8.	19.	*& agam ftudiofiùs,*
and	a. 1. 8.	20.	*&*

I

I will vrge him with greater vehemency,	a. 1.	8. 21.	*contendam ab illo vehementiùs,*
becaufe by your letter I perceiue you haue fo great a will thereunto.	a. 1.	8. 22.	*quòd tantam ex epi-ftola voluntatem eius rei tuam perfpicere videor.*
Vnderftand thus much,	a. 1.	8. 23.	*Hoc te intelligere volo,*
that hee is very grieuoufly offended:	a. 1.	8. 24.	*pergrauiter illum ef-fe offenfum :*
but	a. 1.	8. 25.	*fed*
becaufe	a. 1.	8. 26.	*quia*
I fee no caufe of moment to ground vpon,	a. 1.	8. 27.	*nullam video gra-uem fubeffe caufam,*
I confidently be-leeue,	a. 1.	8. 28.	*magnoperè confido,*
that he will do as he fhould,	a. 1.	8. 29.	*illum fore in officio,*
and	a. 1.	8. 30.	*&*
as we would haue him.	a. 1.	8. 31.	*in noftra poteftate.*
I would haue you imbarque our Sta-tua's and images of *Mercurie,*	a. 1.	8. 32.	*Signa noftra, &* Hermeraclas (a.1.8. 32.a.b.) *velim impo-nas,*
as thou writeft,	a. 1.	8. 32.a	*vt fcribis,*

when

when you can do it moft coueniently,	a. 1. 8. 32. b	*cùm commodiſsim poteris,*
and	a. 1. 8. 33.	*&*
if you fhall find a-ny thing elfe,	a. 1. 8. 34.	*ſi quod aliud (a. 1. 8. 34. a. b.) reperies :*
that is proper for that place,	a. 1. 8. 34. a	*dixior eius loci,*
which you know of,	a. 1. 8. 34. b	*quem non ignoras,*
and	a. 1. 8. 35.	*&*
efpecially	a. 1. 8. 36.	*maximè*
fuch things which you fhall thinke fit for the place of ex-ercife, and Acade-mie.	a. 1. 8. 37.	*quæ tibi paleſtra, gymnaſijque videbun-tur eſſe.*
For	a. 1. 8. 38.	*Etenim*
fitting there, I wrote thefe things vnto thee,	a. 1. 8. 39.	*ibi ſedens hæc ad te ſcribebam,*
that the place might tell me [what I fhould write.]	a. 1. 8. 40.	*vt me locus ipſe ad-moneret.*
Moreouer,	a. 1. 8. 41.	*Præterea,*
I giue you in charge the Images of playfter,	a. 1. 8 . 42.	*typos tibi mando,*

Proprium.

which

which I may fet within the parget-ting of my little hall,	a. 1. 8. 43.	*quos in tettorio atri-oli poſsim includere,*
and	a. 1. 8. 44.	*&*
two couers for Wells, adorned with figurets.	a. 1. 8. 45.	*putealia ſigillata duo.*
Take heed you promife not your Library to any man,	a. 1. 8. 46.	*Bibliothecam tuam caue cuiquam deſpon-deas,*
though you fhould find him neuer fo de-firous thereof:	a. 1. 8. 47.	*quamuis acrem a-matorem inueneris:*
for	a. 1. 8. 48.	*nam*
I keepe all the lit-tle things that I haue gathered together to that purpofe,	a. 1. 8. 49.	*ego omnes meas vin-demiolas eò reſeruo,*
that I might pro-uide that helpe for mine old age.	a. 1. 8. 50.	*vt illud ſubſidium ſenectuti parem.*
Concerning my brother,	a. 1. 8. 51.	*De fratre*
I truft that things doe fo ftand,	a. 1. 8. 52.	*confido ita eſſe,*
as I defired and la-boured they fhould.	a. 1. 8. 53.	*vt ſemper volui & elaboraui.*
There are many tokens thereof,	a. 1. 8. 54.	*Multa ſigna ſunt eius rei,*

[and

[and this is] not the leaſt,	a. 1. 8.55.	*non minimum*
that [your] ſiſter is with childe.	a. 1. 8.56.	*quòd ſoror prægnans eſt.*
About my prefer-ments	a. 1. 8.57.	*De comitijs meis*
I both remember	a. 1. 8.85.	*& (a. 1. 8. 58. a.) memini*
that I haue giuen thee leaue to be abſent,	a. 1. 8.58. a	*tibi me permiſiſſe,*
and alſo	a. 1. 8.59.	*&*
I haue publiſhed as much	a. 1. 8.60.	*ego (a. 1. 8.60.a.) hoc (a. 1. 8.60.b. c.) prædico*
long ſince	a. 1. 8.60. a	*iampridem*
to ſuch as are both our friends,	a. 1. 8.60. b	*communibus ami-cis,*
which expect thee:	a. 1. 8.60. c	*qui te expectant:*
and	a. 1. 8.61.	*&*
I will not only not call thee;	a. 1. 8.62.	*te non modo non ar-ceſſam;*
but	a. 1. 8.63.	*ſed*
I will forbid thee.	a. 1. 8.64.	*prohibebo.*
In that I know	a. 1. 8.65.	*quod intelligam*
that it much more concernes thee	a. 1. 8.66.	*multò magis intereſſe tua*
that thou doe	a. 1. 8.67.	*te agere*

what

what is to bee done,	a. 1.	8.68.	*quod agendum eſt,*
at this time	a. 1.	8.69.	*hoc tempore*
than [it concerns] mee	a. 1.	8.70.	*quàm * mea*
that thou bee pre- ſent at [my] promo- tion.	a. 1.	8.71.	*te adeſſe comitÿs.*
Therefore,	a. 1.	8.72.	*Proinde,*
I would haue thee be of that minde,	a. 1.	8.73.	*eo animo te velim eſ- ſe,*
as if thou were ſent into thoſe places	a. 1.	8.74.	*quaſi* (a.1. 8. 74.a.) *in iſta loca miſſus eſſes*
vpon my occaſions	a. 1.	8.74. a	*mei negotÿ cauſa.*
And	a. 1.	8.75.	(a.1.8.75.a.*autem*
thou ſhalt both finde and heare mee to be that man	a. 1.	8.75. a	*me* (a.1.8.75.) *cum & offendes* (a.1.8.75. b.) *& audies*
towards thee	a. 1.	8.75. b	*erga te*
as if I had atchie- ued things	a. 1.	8.76.	*quaſi,mihi* (a. 1. 8. 76. a. b. c. d.) *parta ſint*
(if any things bee atchieued)	a. 1.	8.76. a	*(ſi qua parta erunt)*
not onely	a. 1.	8.76. b	*non modò*
by thy preſence,	a. 1.	8.76. c	*te praſente,*

intereſſet

but

but	a. 1.	8.76. d	*fed*
through thy pro-curement.	a. 1.	8.76. c	*per te.*
Little *Tullia* fets you a day :	a. 1.	8.67.	Tulliola *tibi diem dat :*
[and] fhee calls vpon[your] furety.	a. 1.	8.68.	*fponforem appellat.*
I haue both for-merly endeauoured [it] of mine owne accord,	a. 1.	9. 1.	*Et mea fponte facie-bam antea,*
and	a. 1.	9. 2.	*&*
fince	a. 1.	9. 3.	*poft*
I am much mo-ued		9. 4.	(a.1.9.4.a.b.) *mag-nopere fum commo-tus*
with two of your epiftles	a. 1.	9. 4.a	*duabus epiftolis tu-is*
written to the fame purpofe, with great diligence.	a. 1.	9. 4.b	*perdiligenter in ean-dem rationem fcri-ptis.*
And befides, *Salu-ftius* was a daily mo-uer	a. 1.	9. 5.	*Eò accedebat horta-tor afsiduus,* Salufti-us
that I fhould deale	a. 1.	9. 6.	*vt agerem*
very diligently	a. 1.	9. 7.	*quàm diligentifsimè*
with *Lucceius*	a 1.	9. 8.	*cum* Lucceio

about the reconci-ling you each to others ancient fauour.	a. 1. 9. 9.	*de veſtra vetere gratia reconcilianda.*
But	a. 1. 9. 10.	*Sed*
when I had don all [I could,]	a. 1. 9. 11.	*cùm omnia jeciſſem,*
I could not onely not recouer the good will he bare thee,	a. 1. 9. 12.	*non modò eam voluntatem eius, quæ fuerat erga te, receperare non potui,*
but	a. 1. 9. 13.	*verùm*
not ſo much as gather the cauſe of his diſtaſte.	a. 1. 9. 14.	*ne cauſam quidem elicere immutatæ voluntatis.*
Although	a. 1. 9. 15.	*Tametſi*
indeede he harpes vpon that award of his, & thoſe things,	a. 1. 5. 16.	*iactat ille quidem illud ſuum arbitrium, & ea,*
which I knew diſguſted him,	a. 1. 9. 17.	*quæ (a. 1. 9. 17. a. b.) offendere eius animum intelligebam,*
euen then,	a. 1. 9. 17. a	*iam tum,*
when you were preſent:	a. 1. 9. 17. b	*cùm aderas:*
yet	a. 1. 9. 18.	*tamen*
queſtionleſſe hee hath ſomething	a. 1. 9. 19.	*habet quiddam profectò*

that hee takes ne-rer to heart:	a. 1.9.20.	*quòd magis in animo eius insederit :*
which neither thy Epistle, nor the commiſſion we had from thee can ſo well put out,	a. 1. 9.21.	*quod neque epistola tua, neque nostra legatio, tam potest facilè delere.*
as you may take [it] away by your preſence,	a. 1.9.22.	*quàm tu præsens* (a. 1.9.22. a.b.c.d.) *tolles*
not onely	a. 1.9.22. a	*non modò*
by cõmunication,	a. 1.9.22. b	*oratione,*
but	a. 1.9.22. c	*ſed*
with that famili-liar countenance of thine,	a. 1.9.22. d	*tuo vultu ille familiari,*
if you ſhall thinke [him] worth it;	a. 1.9.23.	*ſi modò tanti putaris;*
as, aſſuredly you will thinke [him]	a. 1.9.24.	*id quod* (a.1.9.24. r. b.c.) *certè putabis,*
if I may counſell you,	a. 1.9.24. a	*ſi me audies,*
and	a. 1.9.24. b	*&*
if you will bee as courteous as you were wont to be.	a. 1.9.24. c	*ſi humanitati tuæ conſtare voles.*
And	a. 1.9.25.	*Ac*

left you fhould wonder,	a. 1. 9.26.	*ne illud mirere,*
why I fhould now feeme to diftruft the fame,	a. 1. 9.27.	*cur (* a. 1. 9. 27. a. b.c.) *nunc idem videar diffidere,*
hauing formerly fignified vnto thee by letters	a. 1. 9.27. a	*cùm ego antea fignificarem tibi per literas*
that I had hope,	a. 1. 9.27. b	*me fperare,*
that I could doe what wee defired with him.	a. 1. 9.27. c	*illum in noftra poteftate fore.*
It is incredible,	a. 1. 9.28.	*Incredibile eft,*
how much I finde him more obftinate, and confirmed,	a. 1. 9.29.	*quanto mihi videatur illius voluntas obftinatior & (*a 1.9.29. a.) *obfirmatior,*
in this indignation.	a. 1. 9.29. a	*in hac iracundia.*
But	a. 1. 9.30.	*Sed*
thefe things will either bee remedied	a. 1. 9.31.	*hæc aut fanabuntur*
when you come,	a. 1. 9.32.	*cùm veneris,*
or	a. 1. 9.33.	*aut*
they will lye heauy on him,	a. 1. 9.34.	*ei molefta erunt,*

in

in whether foeuer the fault be,	a. 1. 9.35.	*in vtro culpa erit:*
About that which was written in your letter,	a. 1. 9. 36.	*Quod in epiftola tua fcriptum erat,*
that I am already thought	a. 1. 9. 37.	*me iam arbitrari*
to be chofen.	a. 1. 9. 38.	*defignatum effe.*
Know,	a. 1. 9. 39.	*Scito,*
that there is nothing more purfued,	a. 1. 9. 40.	*nihil tam exercitum effe,*
now	a. 1. 9. 41.	*nunc*
at Rome	a. 1. 9. 42.	*Romæ*
with all iniuries,	a. 1. 9. 43.	*(a. 1.9.43.a.) omnibus iniquitatibus,*
than fuch as ftand to bee magiftrates.	a. 1. 9.43. a	*quàm candidatos.*
[And] that it is not knowne,	a. 1. 9.44.	*nec (a.1.9. 44.a.) fciri,*
when the affemblies will bee made for [their] election.	a. 1. 9.44. a	*quando futura fint comitia.*
But	a. 1. 9. 45.	*verùm*
Philadelphus fhall relate thefe things vnto thee.	a. 1. 9.46.	*hæc audies de* Philadelpho.

I

I would haue thee presently send,	a. 1.	9.47.	*Tu velim* (a.1.9.47. a.) *quã primũ mittas,*
the things thou haft prepared for our Academie.	a. 1.	9.47. a	*quæ Academia noſtra paráſti.*
'Tis wonderfull,	a. 1.	9.48.	*Mirum,*
how much, not only the vſe, but alſo the thought of that place delighteth [me.]	a. 1.	9.49.	*quàm illius loci non modò vſus, ſed etiam cogitatio delectat.*
But	a. 1.	9.50.	(a.1.9.50.a.) *verò*
take heede thou deliuer not thy bookes to any man	a. 1.	9.50. a	*libros* (a. 1. 9. 50.) *tuos caue cuiquam tradas.*
Keepe them for vs.	a. 1.	9.51.	*Nobis eos* (a.1.9.51. a.) *conſerua.*
as thou writeſt,	a. 1.	9.51. a	*quemadmodũ ſcribis,*
I am poſſeſt of an exceeding deſire to haue them,	a. 1.	9.52.	*ſummum me eorum ſtudium tenet,*
as I [am poſſeſt] alſo at this preſent of a loathing of all things elſe :	a. 1.	9.53.	*ſicut odium iam cæterarum rerum :*
which, how ſoone, how much worſe you ſhall finde,	a. 1.	9.54.	*quas tu,* (a.1.9.56.a.) *quàm breui tempore, quantò deteriores offenſurus ſis,*

then

than you left [them,]	a. 1. 9. 5 5.	*quàm reliquiſti,*
(it) is incredible.	a. 1. 9. 5 6.	*incredibile eſt.*
That *Teucris,*	a. 1. 9. 5 7.	Teucris *illa,*
[is] inſooth a ſlow buſines.	a. 1. 9. 5 8.	*lentum ſanè negotium.*
Neyther did *Cornelius* afterwards returne vnto *Terentia.*	a. 1. 9. 5 9.	*Neque* Cornelius *ad* Terentiam *poſtea redijt.*
I thinke	a. 1. 9.60.	*Opinor*
wee muſt haue recourſe to *Conſidius, Axius,* and *Selicius.*	a. 1. 9.60. a	*ad* Conſidium, Axium, Selicium *confugiendum eſt.*
For,	a. 1. 9. 61.	*Nam,*
from *Cecilius,* his kindred cannot procure mony vnder 12.in the 100.	a. 1. 9. 62.	*à* Cæcilio *propinqui minore* ᵃ*centeſimus nūmum mouere non poſſunt.*
But	a. 1. 9.63.	*Sed*
to returne where we left:	a. 1. 9.64.	*vt ad prima illa redeam:*
I haue not ſeene a more impudēt, crafty or ſlow thing than ſhee is.	a. 1. 9.65.	*nihil ego illa impudentius aſtutius, lentius vidi.*

foeneratores & diuites.

ᵃ ſingulis ſcil: menſibus

Theſe

[Thefe words] I fend[my] free man.	a. 1.	9.66.	*Libertum mitto.*
I haue giuen order to *Titius.*	a. 1.	9.67.	Titio *mandaui.*
[are nothing but] excufes and delays,	a. 1.	9.68.	σκη΄ψις atque ἀναβολαὶ.
but	a. 1.	9.69.	*fed*
I know not.	a. 1.	9.70.	*nefcio*
whether fortune deale better for vs thē we for our felues	a. 1.	9.71.	an* ταυτόματον ἡμῶ᷄, & c :
For	a. 1.	9. 72.	*Nam*
the Currier's of *Pompeius* giue me to vnderftand,	a. 1.	9.73.	*mihi* Pompeiani *prodromi nuntiant,*
that *Pompeius* will openly declare,	a. 1.	9.74.	*apertè Pompeium acturum,*
that *Antonius* muft haue another in his place :	a. 1.	9.75.	Antonio *fuccedi oportere :*
and at the fame time	a. 1.	9. 76.	*eodémque tempore*
the Pretor will propound it to the people.	a. 1.	9.77.	*aget prætor ad populum,*
The bufineffe is of that nature,	a. 1.	9.78.	*Res eiufmodi eft,*

excufationes & dilationes

* pars. verfus Menandri, euius fenfus: *Cafus nofter,* &c. (fubaudi) melius confultet quam nos ipfi,

that|

that I cannot with my reputation defend the man, and hold my esteeme, either with such as are good, or with the people,	a. 1. 9.79.	*vt ego nec per bonos nec per popularem exiſtimationem honeſtè poſsim hominem defendere,*
neither will it bee lawfull for me,	a. 1. 9.80.	*nec mihi libeat,*
which is more then all the reſt.	a. 1. 9.81.	*quod vel maximum eſt.*
For	a. 1. 9.82.	*Etenim*
this hath happened,	a. 1. 9.83.	*accidit hoc,*
which whatſoeuer it be I wholly ſend you,	a. 1. 9.84.	*quod totum cuiuſmodi ſit, mando tibi*
that you may well informe your ſelfe [thereof.]	a. 1. 9.85.	*vt perſpicias.*
I haue a ſlaue made free, in ſooth a wicked fellow,	a. 1. 9.86.	*Libertum ego habeo, ſanè nequam hominem,*
I meane *Hilarus* your Auditor and retainer.	a. 1. 9.87.	*Hilarum dico, ratiocinatorem & clientem tuum.*

Con-

Concerning him *Valerius* the Interpretour fends mee word,	a. 1.	9.88.	*De eo mihi* Valerius *Interpres nuntiat,*
and *Chilius* writes hee heard thefe things:	a. 1.	9.89.	Chiliúfque *fe audiffe fcribit hæc* :
that the fellow is with *Antonius.*	a. 1.	9.90.	*effe hominem cum* Antonio.
And further	a. 1.	9.91.	(a. 1. 9. 91.a.) *porrò*
that *Antonius* in gathering the money often reporteth,	a. 1.	9.91. a	Antonium (a. 1. 9. 91.) *in cogendis pecunijs diclitare,*
that a part thereof is collected for me.	a. 1.	9.92.	*partem mihi queri,*
and	a. 1.	9.93.	*&*
that I haue fent my free'd flaue to be keeper of the common gaine.	a. 1.	9.94.	*à me cuftodem communis quæftus libertũ effe miffum.*
I was not a little moued,	a. 1.	9.95.	*Non fum mediocriter commotus,*
and yet I gaue no credit [thereunto:]	a. 1.	9.96.	*neque tamen credidi:*
But	a. 1.	9.97.	*fed*
doubtleffe,	a. 1.	9.98.	*certè,*

there

there hath beene some fpeech [about it.]	a. 1. 9.99.	*aliquid fermonis fuit.*
fearch out the whole matter, informe your felfe, & looke well to it,	a. 1.9.100.	*totum inueftiga, cognofce, perfpice,*
and	a. 1.9.101.	*&*
remoue that knaue from thence,	a. 1.9. 102.	*nebulonem illum (a. 1.9. 102. a.) ex iftis locis ámoue.*
if you can by any meanes,	a. 1.9.102.a	*fi quo pacto potes,*
Valerius named *Cneius Plancius* author of this fpeech.	a. 1.9.103.	*Huius fermonis* Valerius *autorem* * Cn: Plancium *nominabat.*
I charge you, in any cafe,	a. 1.9.104.	*mando tibi planè,*
that you examine the whole matter how it ftands.	a. 1.9.105.	*totum vt videas cuiufmodi fit.*
It is manifeft that *Pompeius* beares vs great affedion.	a. 1.9.106.	Pompeium *nobis amicifsimum* conftat *effe.*
The diuorce of *Mucia* is much approued.	a. 1.9.107.	*Diuortium* Muciæ *vehementer probatur.*

* Cncium.

I

I suppose you haue heard, how *Publius Clodius*, sonne of *Appius*, hath beene found in womans apparell,	a. 1.	9.108.	*P. Clodium, Appij* F. *te credo audiſſe cum veſte muliebri deprehenſum*,
In the houſe of *Caius Cæſar*,	a. 1.	9.109.	*Domi C.* Cæſaris,
when [the ſacrifice] was made for the people,	a. 1.	9.110.	*Cùm pro populo fieret*,
and how hee was ſaued and convayed away by meanes of a maideſlaue :	a. 1.	9.111.	*eúmque per manus ſeruulæ ſeruatum, & eductum :*
[and] that it is a matter of great infamy :	a. 1.	9.112.	*rem eſſe inſigni infamiâ :*
which I am aſſured.	a. 1.	9.113.	*quod* (a.1.9.113.a.) *certò ſcio.*
that you take haynouſly,	a. 1.	9.113.a	*te moleſtè ferre,*
I haue nothing elſe to write vnto you,	a. 1.	9.114.	*Quod præterea ad te ſcribam non habeo,*
and,	a. 1.	9.115.	*&,*
in good earneſt,	a. 1.	9.116.	*mehercule,*

* Publium.
* Filium.
* Caij.

I

I was much troub-led when I wrote:	a. 1. 9.117.	*eram in scribendo conturbatior :*
For	a. 1. 9.118.	*Nam*
Sositheus a very pleasant childe and one that read vnto vs, dyed;	a. 1. 9.119.	*puer festiuus, anagno-stes noster,* Sosithe-us, *decess.rat ;*
and it moued mee more	a. 1. 9.120.	*méque plus (a. 1.9. 120. a.) commouerat*
thē it was thought a seruants death should.	a. 1. 9.120.a	*quàm serui mors de-bere videbatur.*
I would haue thee often write vnto vs.	a. 1. 9.121.	*Tu velim sæpè ad nos scribas.*
If you shall haue nothing,	a. 1. 9.122.	*si rem nullam habe-bis,*
write whatsoeuer comes into your minde.	a. 1. 9.123.	*quod in buccam ve-nerit, scribito.*
fare well.	a. 1. 9.124.	*vale.*
on the Kalends of Ianuary.	a. 1. 9.125.	*Kalendis Ian.*
in the Consulships of Marcus Messalla, and Marcus Piso.	a. 1. 9.126.	M. Messalla, & M. Pisone. Coss.
I haue now recei ued three of thine epistles :	a. 1. 10. 1.	*Accepi tuas treis iam epistolas:*

Ianuarij

M. ⌠Mar-
M. ⌡co
Cos. Con-
sulibus.

one

one from *Marcus Cornelius,*	a. 1.	10. 2.	*vnam à* M. Cornelio,	Sc:epistolas accepi
which thou gauest him at the three Tauernes :	a. 1.	10. 3.	*quam à tribus ei tabernis (*a. 1. 10.3.a.*) dedisti :*	
(as I suppose)	a. 1.	10.3. a	*(vt opinor)*	
another,	a. 1.	10. 4.	*alteram,*	Sc:epistolas accepi
which your Host *Canusinus* brought me;	a. 1.	10. 5.	*quam mihi* Canusinus, *tuus hospes, reddidit;*	
The third	a. 1.	10. 6.	*Tertiam,*	Sc:epistolas accepi
which thou sent'st from the barke:	a. 1.	10. 7.	*quam (*a.1 10.7.a.b.*) de phaselo dedisti:*	
after the ankers were wayed	a. 1.	10.7. a	*anchoris solutis*	
(as thou writest)	a. 1.	10.7. b	*(ut scribis)*	
which were all full of Rhethoricke.	a. 1.	10. 8.	*quæ fuerunt omnes Rethorum.*	
their stile is pure	a. 1.	10. 9.	*purè loquntur,*	
both	a. 1.	10.10.	*Cùm*	
seasoned with humanity,	a. 1.	10.11.	*humanitatis sparsa sale,*	
and	a. 1.	10.12.	*tùm*	
for tokens of loue, worth the noting.	a 1.	10.13.	*insignes amoris notis.*	
By which Letters	a. 1.	10.14.	*Quibus epistolis*	

I

I am indeede pro-uokoe by you	a. 1.	10.15.	*ſum equidem abs te laceſsitus*
to write backe a-gaine :	a. 1.	10.15.a	*ad reſcribendum :*
But	a. 1.	10.16.	*ſed*
the reaſon of my ſlackeneſſe is ,	a. 1.	10.17.	*idcirco cum tardior,*
that I cannot finde a truſty meſſenger.	a. 1.	10.18.	*quòd non inuenio fi-delem tabellarium.*
for who is he,	a. 1.	10.19.	*quotus enim quiſque eſt,*
that is able to carry a Letter of any weight,	a. 1.	10.20.	*qui epiſtolam paulò grauiorem ferre poſsit,*
vnleſſe, he make it lighter by reading it?	a. 1.	10.21.	*niſi eam per lectionem releuerit ?*
Whereunto may be added,	a. 1.	10.22.	*Accedit eò,*
that I haue not knowne,	a. 1.	10. 23.	*quòd mihi non eſt no-tum,*
that any ſhould go into Epirus or Alba-nia.	a. 1.	10. 24.	*vt quiſque in Epirum proficiſcatur.*
For I ſuppoſe'd thee	a. 1.	10. 25.	*ego enim te arbitror*

(the

(the sacrifices made in thine *Amalthea,*)	a. 1.	10.26.	(*cæsis apud* Amaltheā *tuam victimis,*)
to bee presently gone:	a. 1.	10. 27.	*Statim esse* (a.1. 10. 27.a.)*profectum:*
to assault Sicyon:	a. 1.	10.27.a	*ad Sicyonem oppugnandum :*
and yet I am not certaine thereof,	a. 1.	10.28.	*neque id ipsum tamen certum habeo,*
when thou wilt go to *Antonie,*	a. 1.	10. 29.	*quando ad* Antoniū *proficiscare,*
or	a. 1.	10.30.	*aut*
how long thou wilt abide in Epirus.	a. 1.	10.31.	*quid in* Epiro *temporis ponas.*
So that	a. 1.	10.32.	*Ita*
I dare not trust letters, in which I am a little freer then ordinarie , neyther with men of *Achaia,* nor of Epirus.	a. 1.	10.33.	*neque* Achaicis *hominibus, neque* Epiroticis *paulò liberiores litteras committere audeo.*
Yet there are thing worth the writing [happened]	a. 1.	10.34.	*sunt autem* (a. 1. 10. 34.a.)*res digna literis nostris*

since

ſince thou went'ſt from me:	a. 1. 10.34.a	*poſt diſceſſum à me tuum :*
but,	a. 1. 10.35.	*ſed,*
not to be committed to ſuch hazard,	a. 1. 10.36.	*non committendæ eiuſmodi periculo,*
as to bee eyther loſt, opened, or intercepted.	a. 1. 10. 37.	*vt aut interire, aut aperiri, aut intercipi poſsint.*
Firſt therfore thou ſhalt know ,	a. 1. 10.38.	*Primùm igitur ſcito,*
that I was not firſt asked mine opinion,	a. 1. 10.39.	*primum * me non eſſe * rogatum ſententiam,*
and that he which pacified the Allobroges was put before vs,	a. 1. 10.40.	*præpoſitúmque eſſe nobis pacificatorem Allobrogum,*
not without the murmuring of the Senate,	a. 1. 10.41.	*idque admurmurante ſenatu,*
and that it was not done againſt my will	a. 1. 10.42.	*neque me inuito eſſe factum*
for	a. 1. 10.43.	*(a. 1. 10. 43.a.) enim*

* vt Senatus principem * à M. Piſone Conſule.

I

I am [by this meanes] freed,	a. 1.	10.43.a	*ſum*(a.1.10.43.b. c.) *liber*,
both	a. 1.	10.43.b	*&*
from obſeruing a peruerſe man,	a. 1.	10.43.c	*ab obſeruando homine peruerſo*,

Sc:M.Piſon Conſule.

and alſo	a. 1.	10.44.	*&*
[I am] at liberty to doe what may ſtand with my reputation in the common wealth,	a. 1.	10.45.	*ad dignitatem in repub: retinendam* (a. 1.10.45.a.) *ſolutus*,

Sc:Sum. republica

whether hee will or no	a. 1.	10.45.a	*contra illius voluntatem*
and	a. 1.	10.46.	*&*
that ſecond place in giuing the opinion hath almoſt equal authority with him that is firſt.	a. 1.	10.47.	*ille ſecundus in dicendo locus habet auctoritatem pænè principis.*
and	a. 1.	10.48.	*&*
is not too much tyed vnto the Conſuls fauour	a. 1.	10.49.	*voluntatem non nimis deuinctã beneficio coſ.*

Sc:Habet Coſ.Conſulis.

The third is *Catulus.*	a. 1.	10.50.	*tertius eſt* Catulus.
the fourth *Hortenſius.*	a. 1.	10.51.	*quartus*(a.1.10.51.a.) Hortenſius.

Sc: eſt

if

(if you defire [to know] this alfo)	a. 1.	10.51.a	(*fi etiam hoc quæris*)
but	a. 1.	10.52.	(a.1.10.52. a.) *autem*
the Confull him-felfe [is] of a weake and wicked fpirit :	a. 1.	10.52.a	**Cof.* (a. 1. 10. 52.) *ipfe paruo animo, & prauo:*	*Cof.Conful.
only a wrangler	a. 1.	10.53.	*tantùm cauillator*
in that wayward fafhion,	a. 1.	10.54.	*genere illo morofo,*
that is laught at, though it were without fcoffery:	a. 1.	10.55.	*quod etiam fine dicacitate ridetur:*
being ridiculous rather for face, then for his iefts :	a. 1.	10.56.	*facie magis, quàm facetÿs ridiculus :*
doing nothing in the common wealth but what the great ones will :	a. 1.	10.57.	*nihil agens in*rep: feiunctus ab optimatibus :*	*republica.
from whom	a. 1.	10.58.	*à quo*
thou canft hope for no good to the common weale,	a. 1.	10.59.	*nihil fperes boni *reipub.*	*reipublicæ.
becaufe hee will not :	a. 1.	10.60.	*quia non vult :*
thou need'ft feare no ill,	a. 1.	19.61.	*nihil metuas mali,*

be-

becaufe hee dares not.	a. 1. 10.62.	*quia non audet.*
But his colleague	a. 1. 10.63.	*Eius autem collega*
both	a. 1. 10 64.	*&*
honours me much	a. 1. 10.65.	*in me perbonorifi- cus,*
and	a. 1. 10.66.	*&*
fauours fuch as are of the good fa- ction, and defends them.	a. 1. 10.67.	*partium ſtudioſus, ac defenſor bonarum.*
And that which is more	a. 1. 10.68.	*Quinimò*
they are fcarce ca- ter-coufins.	a. 1. 10.69.	*leuiter inter ſe diſsi- dent.*
But	a. 1. 10.70.	*Sed*
I feare,	a. 1. 10.71.	*vereor,*
that this will fefter farther,	a. 1. 10.72.	*ne hoc (a. 1. 10. 72. a.) ſerpat longi- ùs,*
which is infected,	a. 1. 10.72.a	*quod infectum eſt,*
for	a. 1. 10.73.	*(a.1.10.73. a.)enim*
I beleeue	a. 1. 10.73.a	*credo*
that you haue heard,	a 1. 10.74.	*te audiſſe,*
whilft the facrifices were made for the peoples fafety,	a. 1. 10. 75.	*cùm (a 1.10. 75. a.) pro populo fieret,* Serres diuinæ Bonæ Deæ.

at

at *Cefars*,	a. 1.	10.75.a	*apud* Cæfarem,
that there came a man in womans apparell:	a. 1.	10.76.	*veniſſe eò muliebri veſtitu virum:*
and the Virgins hauing reſtored that ſacrifice,	a. 1.	10.77.	*ídque ſacrificium cũ Virgines inſtauràſſent,*
that *Quintus Cornificius* made mention thereof:	a. 1.	10.78.	*mentionẽ à* Q.Cornificio(a.1.10.78.a.) *factam:*
in the Senate	a. 1.	10.78.a	*in ſenatu*
(he was the firſt,	a. 1.	10.79.	*(is fuit princeps,*
left thou might'ſt peraduenture thinke it to be ſome one of vs)	a. 1.	10.80.	*ne tu fortè aliquem noſtrum putes)*
afterwards	a. 1.	10.81.	*poſtea*
that the matter was referred to the Virgins , and the Pontifices,	a. 1.	10.82.	*rem (a.1.10.82.a.) ad virgines, atque ad pontifices relatam,*
by the Senats decree	a. 1.	01.82.a	*ex* * S. * C.

vt pollutum

Q. Quinto.

* Senatus
* Confulto.

and

and that it was de-cree'd by them to be a wicked deede :	a. 1.	1 0.83.	*idque ab ijs nefas esse decretum :*
And then	a. 1.	1 0.84.	*Deinde*
that the Consuls had published the copie or president of the lawe ;	a. 1.	1 0.85.	(a.1.10.85.a.)*consules* [a] *rogationem promulgasse;*
by the Senats order.	a. 1.	1 0.85.a	*ex* * *S.* * *C.*
and that *Cæsar* had sent back to his wife a bill or letter [of diuorce,]	a. 1.	1 0.86.	[a] *Vxori* Cæsarem * *nuntium remisisse*
In this businesse	a. 1.	1 0.87.	*In hac causa*
Piso laboureth,	a. 1.	1 0.88.	Piso(a.1.10.88.a.) *operam dat,*
being led by the friendship of *Publius Clodius,*	a. 1.	1 0.88.a	*amicitia* * Pub.Clodij *ductus,*
that the same law should bee abolished.	a. 1.	1 0.89.	*vt ea rogatio*(a.1.89. a.b.c.)*antiquetur.*
which he propoundeth, and propoundeth by order of the Senate.	a. 1.	1 0.89.a	*quam ipse fert, & fert ex* *S.* *C.*
and	a. 1.	1 0.89.b	*&*

Marginal notes:

[a] Vt iudicium de pollutis Sacris constitueretur.
* Senatus * Consulto

[a] Pompeia * repudij: se

* Publij

* Senatus * Consulto.

in

in matter of Religion,	a. 1. 10.89.c	*de religione,*
Mesalla hitherto goes very seuerely to worke.	a. 1. 10. 90.	[a]*Mesalla vehementer adhuc agit * seuerè.*
The good men leaue the businesse.	a. 1. 10.91.	*boni viri (a. 1. 10. 92. a.) remouentur à causa.*
moued by the intreaties of *Clodius.*	a. 1. 10.91.a	*precibus* Clodij
such as are wrought, are gathered together.	a. 1. 10.92.	*operæ comparantur.*
wee our selues are daily mitigated.	a. 1. 10. 93.	*nosmetipsi, (a. 1. 10. 94. a.) quotidiè demitigamur.*
who had from the beginning been *Lycurgeans.*	a. 1. 10.93.a	*qui * Lycurgei à principio fuissemus.*
Cato stands for him,	a. 1. 10.94.	*Instat (a. 1.10.95.a. b.)* Cato,
and	a. 1. 10.94 a	*&*
he is earnest.	a. 1. 10.94.b	*vrget.*

Marginal notes:
[a] Consul et seuerè.
[*] Legis de de pollutis sacris quasi latores, vt Lycurgus.

what

what needs man words? [or] In a word	a. 1.	10.95.	*quid multa?*
I feare,	a. 1.	10.96.	*vereor,*
that thefe things neglected by the good, and defended by the wicked, may prooue the caufe of great mifchiefes to the Common wealth.	a. 1.	10.97.	*ne hæc neglecta à bo-nis, defenfa ab impro-bis, magnorum*reipub. malorum caufa fit.*
but	a. 1.	10. 98.	*(a. 1. 10. 99.a.) au-tem*
that friend of thine,	a. 1.	10.98.a	*tuus (a. 1. 10.99.) ille amicus,*
knowft thou whom I meane?	a. 1.	10.99.	*fcin' quem dicam?*
of whom thou wrot'ft vnto me,	a. 1.	10.100.	*de quo tu ad me fcrip-fifti,*
that, feeing hee durft not repre-hend,	a. 1.	10.101.	*pofteaquàm non au-deret reprehendere,*
he began to com-mend:	a. 1.	10.75.a	*laudare cœpiffe:*

* *reipublica*

he

he beares great af-fection, embraceth and makes much of vs, commends vs o-penly, priuately en-uies vs,	a. 1. 10.103.	*nos* (a.1.10.103.a.) *admodum diligit, am-plectitur, amat, aper-tè laudat; occultè* (a.1. 10. 103.b. c.) *inui-det,*
(in shew)	a. 1. 10.103.a	(*ut ostendit*)
(but so,	a. 1. 10.103.b	(*sed ita,*
that it may be well perceiued)	a. 1. 10. 103.c	*vt perspicuum sit*)
nothing is courte-ously [done]	a. 1. 10.104	*nihil come,*
nothing in since-ritie,	a. 1. 10.105	*nihil simplex,*
nothing honestly carried in publike businesse.	a. 1. 10.106.	*nihil* * ἐν τοῖς πολιτικοῖς, *honestum,*
nothing nobly,	a. 1. 10.107.	*nibil illustre,*
nothing with cou-rage, stoutly,	a. 1. 10.108.	*nihil forte,*
nothing freely.	a. 1. 10.109.	*nihil liberum.*
But,	a. 1. 10.110.	*Sed,*
of those things I will write more particularly hereaf-ter.	a. 1. 10.111.	*hæc ad te scribam a-liàs subtilius.*

* *in cladibus.*

for,

For,	a. 1.	1 0.1 1 2.	*Nam,*
neyther to me are they as yet sufficiently knowne,	a. 1.	1 0.1 1 3.	*neque adhuc mihi satis nota sunt,*
and	a. 1.	1 0.1 1 4.	*&*
I dare not commit my letters to this obscure & vnknown fellow.	a. 1.	1 0.1 1 5.	*huic terræ filio, nescio cui, committere epistolam* (a. 1. 10. 115. a.) *non audeo.*
of so waighty matters,	a. 1.	1 0. 1 1 5. a	*tantis de rebus*
The Pretors haue not yet drawne lots for the Prouinces.	a. 1.	1 0. 1 1 6.	*Prouincias prætores nondum sortiti sunt.*
things stand so,	a. 1.	1 0. 1 1 7.	*res eodem est loci,*
as thou left'st them	a. 1.	10. 1 1 8.	*quo reliquisti*
The description of Misenum, and Puteoli, I will include within mine Oration.	a. 1.	1 0. 1 1 9.	* περιγραφὴν, (a. 1. 10. 108. a.) Miseni, & Puteolorum, *includam orationi meæ.*
which thou desirest,	a. 1.	10. 1 1 9. a	*quam postulas,*
I found that on the third of the Nones of December was false written.	a. 1.	1 0.1 2 0·	*ad.* *III. No. Dec. *mendosè fuisse animaduerteram.*

*Loci descriptionem.

*Terentium Nonarum Decembris.

Those

Thofe things which you commended in the orations did greatly pleafe me:	a. 1. 10.121.	quæ laudas ex orationibus (a.1.10.120.a.) valdè mihi placebant :
(beleeue me)	a. 1. 10.121.a	(mihi crede)
But,	a. 1. 10.122.	Sed,
I durft not fay [fo much] before.	a. 1. 10.123.	non audebam anteà dicere.
But now,	a. 1. 10.124.	Nunc verò,
that they are approued by thee,	a. 1. 10.125.	quòd à te probata funt,
they feeme to mee to bee much neerer the Atticke ftyle.	a. 1. 10.126.	multò mi * ατ]ικωτερα videntur.
In that Oration [againft] Metellus	a. 1. 10.127.	In illam orationem Metellinam
I haue added fomthing.	a. 1. 10.128.	addidi quædam.
The booke fhall be fent vnto you,	a. 1. 10.129.	liber tibi mittetur,
becaufe	a. 1. 10.130.	quoniam
the loue you beare vs hath made you a friend to rethoricke.	a. 1. 10.131.	te amor noftri * φιλο-ρίτορα reddidit.
What newes fhall I write you?	a. 1. 10.132.	Noui tibi quidnam fcribam ?
What? [is there any?]	a 1. 10.133.	Quid?

* magis Attica.

* Rhetoricæ Studiofum.

Sc:Supereft.

yes

Yes [there is.]	a. 1.	10.134.	*Etiam.*
The Conful *Meſſalla* hath bought the houſe of *Autronius* for 437. Seſtertij.	a. 1.	10.135.	Meſalla *Coſ.* Autronianam *domum emit* **HS,** CCCC XXX VII.
what's that to me,	a. 1.	10.136.	*Quid id ad me,*
fayſt thou?	a. 1.	10.137.	*inquies?*
Only [thus much,]	a. 1.	10.138.	*Tantum,*
that we are both iudged to haue made a good bargaine:	a. 1.	10.139.	*quòd* (a. 1. 10. 139.a) *& nos benè emiſſe iudicati ſumus:*
by that purchaſe,	a. 1.	10.139. a	*ea emptione,*
and alſo	a. 1.	10.140.	*&*
men haue begun to vnderſtand,	a. 1.	10.141.	*homines intelligere cœperunt,*
that it is lawfull	a. 1.	10.142.	*licère*
to come to ſome degree of honour with the helpe of [our] friends.	a. 1.	10.143.	*amicorum facultatibus* (a.1. 10.142. a.) *ad dignitatem aliquam peruenire.*
In purchaſing,	a. 1.	10.143.a	*In emendo,*
That Teucris,	a. 1.	10.144.	*Teucris illa,*
is a ſlow buſineſſe,	a. 1.	10.145.	*lentum negotium,*

but

but yet,	a. 1.	10.146.	*sed tamen,*
there is hope ther-of.	a. 1.	10.147.	*est in spe.*
Dispatch you these things :	a. 1.	10.148.	*Tu ista confice :*
[and] expect a larger letter from vs.	a. 1.	10.149.	*à nobis liberiorem e-pistolam expecta.*
Farewell.	a. 1.	10.150.	*Vale.*
the 6. of the ka-lends of Februa-ry :	a. 1.	10.151	**VI. Kalendas Feb.*
in the Consulships of Marcus *Messalla,* and Marcus *Piso.*	a. 1.	10.152.	*M. Messalla & M. Pisone*Coss.*
I feare,	a. 1.	11. 1.	*Vereor,*
it may prooue di-staffull,	a. 1.	11. 2.	*ne putidum sit,*
to write vnto thee,	a. 1.	11. 3.	*scribere ad te,*
how full of busi-nesse I am :	a. 1.	11. 4.	*quàm sim occupatus:*
but yet,	a. 1.	11. 5.	*sed tamen,*
I was so hindred by imployments,	a. 1.	11. 6.	*ita distinebar,*
that I had scarce time to write this little letter,	a. 1.	11. 7.	*vt vix huic tantulæ epistolæ tempus habue-rim,*

* Sexto Ka-lendas Fe-bruarias.

*Consulibus.

and

and that (time which I had, was) ftolne from affaires of greateſt importance.	a. 1.	11. 8.	*atque id ereptum è ſummis occupationibus.*
What Pompeius firſt ſpeech was,	a. 1.	11. 9.	*Prima*concio* Pompeij *qualis fuiſſet,*
I haue formerly written vnto you:	a. 1.	11.10.	*ſcripſi ad te antea :*
not pleaſing to ſuch as were in miſery,	a. 1.	11.11.	*non iucunda miſeris,*
in vaine to ſuch as were wicked,	a. 1.	11.12.	*inanis improbis,*
not gratefull to the happy,	a. 1.	11.13.	*beatis non grata,*
not graue to thoſe that were good.	a. 1.	11.14.	*bonis non grauis.*
Therefore	a. 1.	11.15.	*Itaque*
he grew cold :	a. 1.	11.15.a	*frigebat :*
Then,	a. 1.	11. 16.	*Tum,*
by the incitement of the Conſull Piſo.	a. 1.	11. 17.	Piſonis *Cos.*impulſu*

*poſt redi tum,

*Conſuli

Lu-

Lucius Fusius a a. I. 11.18. light-headed Tribune of the people, brought *Pompeius* to the place where he was to fpeake vnto the people.		*leuifsimus Tribunus* *pl.* *L.* Fufius *in concionem produxit* Pōpeium. *pl.plebis* *L.Lucius.*
The thing was acted in the roundell of *Flaminius:*	a. I. 11.19.	*Res agebatur in Circo* Flaminio:
and	a. I. 11.20.	*&*
the affembly was.	a. I. 11.21.	*erat* (a1.11.21.a.b.) *παπήγυεις.* *Conuentus.*
in the fame place,	a. I. 11.21.a	*in eo ipfo loco,*
on the very market day,	a. I. 11.21.b	*ipfo die nundinarum,*
hee demanded of him,	a. I. 11.22.	*quæfiuit ex eo,*
whether it pleafed him,	a. I. 11.23.	*placerétne ei,*
that Comiffioners fhould bee chofen by the Prætor,	a. I. 11. 24.	*iudices à Prætore legi,*
to affift the fayd Prætor.	a. I. 11.25.	*quo confilio idem Prætor vteretur.*
For fo it was ordered,	a. I. 11. 26.	*Id autem erat* (a. I. 11.29.a.b.) *conftitutum,*

con-

concerning the Clodian religion,	a. 1.	11.26.a	*de Clodiana religione,*
by the Senate.	a. 1.	11.26.b	*ab senatu.*
Then	a. 1.	11.27.	*Tum*
Pompeius spake very effectually in the behalfe of the Nobility,	a. 1.	11.28.	Pompeius * μάλ' ἀριστοκρατικῶς *locutus est,* [* valdè pro statu optimatum.]
and	a. 1.	11.29.	(a.1. 11. 30.a.) *que*
he answered,	a. 1.	11.30.	(a.1.11.30.d.) *respondit,*
that hee thought that the Senats authority was the greatest	a. 1.	11.30.a	*Senatus* (a.1.11.29.) *auctoritatem sibi* (a.1. 11.30.b.) *maximam videri,*
in all affaires,	a. 1.	11.30.b	*omnibus in rebus,*
and	a. 1.	11.30.c	(a.1.11.30.d.) *que*
that hee was euer of that mynde	a. 1.	11.30.d	*semper* (a. 1. 11. 30. c.) *visam esse* (a. 1.11.30.)
and	a. 1.	11.31.	*&*
this hee handled at large.	a. 1.	11.32.	*id multis verbis.*
After this	a. 1.	11.33.	*Postea*
Messalla the Consul demanded of *Pompeius* in the Senate,	a 1.	11.34.	Messalla * *Cos.in Senatu de* Pompeio *quæsiuit,* [* Consul]

what

what he thought,	a. 1.	11.35.	*quid* (a. 1.11.35.a. b.c.) *sentiret,*
concerning the religion,	a. 1.	11.35.a	*de religione,*
and	a. 1.	11.35.b	*&*
concerning the law propoſed [or, concerning the order proclaimed]	a. 1.	11.35.c	*de promulgata rogatione*
He ſo ſpake	a. 1.	11.36.	*Locutus ita eſt*
in the Senate,	a. 1.	11.36.a	*in ſenatu,*
that hee generally commended all the decrees of that order:	a.1.	11.37.	*vt omnia illius ordinis conſulta* * χαπικοῖς *laudaret :*
and	a. 1.	11.38.	(a. 1.11.38.a.) *que*
he ſaide to me	a. 1.	11.38.a	*mihi* (a.1.11.38.)b.) *dixit,*
as he ſate by [me]	a. 1.	11.38.b	*vt aſſedit,*
that he thought		11.39.	*ſe putare*
that he had ſufficiently anſwered.	a. 1.	11.40.	*ſatis ab ſe* (a. 1. 11. 40. a.) *eſſe reſponſum.*
Concerning theſe matters alſo,	a. 1.	11.40.a	*Etiam de iſtis rebus,*
Craſſus aroſe	a.1.	11. 41.	Craſſus (a. 1. 11. 41.a.b.c. d.e.) *ſurrexit,*

*generaliter.

ha-

hauing perceiued	a. 1.	11.41. a	*posteaquàm vidit*
that he had recei- ued commendati- on	a. 1.	11.41.b	*illum excepisse lau- dem*
thereby,	a. 1.	10.41.c	*ex eo,*
in that these men perceiued,	a. 1.	11.41.d	*quòd hi suspicarentur homines,*
that my Consul- ship pleased him,	a. 1.	11.41.c	*ei consulatum meum placere,*
and	a. 1.	11. 42.	*(a.1.11.42.a)que*
he spake most ho- nourably	a. 1.	11.42. a	*ornatissimè (a.1.11. 42.)b.) locutus est*
of my Consul- ship,	a. 1.	11.42.b	*de meo consulatu,*
saying	a. 1.	11.43.	*vt(a.1.11.43.a.)diceret*
after this manner,	a. 1.	11.43.a	*ita*
that hee acknow- ledged that it pro- ceeded from me :		11. 44.	*se(a.1. 11.44. a. b. c. d.) mihi acceptum referre :*
that hee was a Se- natour,	a. 1.	11.44.a	*quòd esset senatro,*
that a Citizen,	a. 1.	11.44.b	*quòd ciuis,*
that a freeman,	a. 1.	11.44.c	*quòd liber,*
that he liued,	a. 1.	11.44.d	*quòd viueret,*
as oft as he beheld his wife, his house, his Countrey,	a. 1.	11.45.	*quoties coniugē, quo- ties domum, quoties pa- triam videret,*

so

ſo often	a. 1. 11.46.	*totiès*
that he ſaw my good office.	a. 1. 11.47.	*ſe beneficium meum videre.*
What needs many words?	a. 1. 11.48.	*Quid multa?*
Hee handled with great grauity all that place.	a. 1. 11.49.	*totum hūc locū, (.a. 1. 11.47.a.d.e.f.) valdè grauiter pertexuit.*
which I am wont in perſon of the beſt Citizen to paint out variouſly,	a. 1. 11.49.a	*quem in Ariſtocratia ego variè (a.1.11. 49. b. c. ſoleo pingere,*
in mine Orations	a. 1. 11.49.b	*meis orationibus*
whereof thou art an *Ariſtarchus,* [or, a ſeuere cenſurer,]	a. 1. 11.49.c	*quarum tu* Ariſtarch*us,*
of fire,	a. 1. 11.49.d	*de flamma,*
of ſword,	a. 1. 11.49.e	*de ferro,*
(thou knoweſt thoſe viols or pots,) [from whence I haue that painting,]	a. 1. 11.49.f	*(noſti illas * λκπιθκε.)*
I ſate next vnto *Pompeius:*	a. 1. 11.50.	*Proximus* Pompeio *ſedebam:*
I perceiued,	a. 1. 11.51.	*int llexi,*
the man was moued,	a. 1. 11.52.	*hominem moueri,*

ampullas, i.e. copiam dicendi informem.

whether

whether [it were]	a. 1.	11.53.	*vtrùm*
that *Craſſus* crept into that fauour,	a. 1.	11.54.	*Craſſum inire eam gratiam,*
which he had o- uerſlipped,	a. 1.	11.55.	*quam ipſe prætermi- ſiſſet,*
or,	a. 1.	11.56.	*an,*
that the things that I had done were of that mo- ment,	a. 1.	11.57.	*eſſe tantas res noſtras,*
that they ſhould be commended :	a. 1.	11. 58.	*quæ (a. 1.11.58.a.) laudarentur:*
with ſo great a li- king of the Se- nate,	a. 1.	11.58.a	*tam libenti Senatu,*
of him	a. 1.	11.59.	*ab eo*
eſpecially,	a. 1.	11.60.	*præſertim,*
who ought mee that commendati- on,	a. 1.	11.61.	*qui mibi laudem il- lam(a.1.11.61.a.)de- beret,*
ſo much the leſſe,	a. 1.	11.61. a	*eò minus,*
that in all my writings hee was ſharpely touched.	a. 1.	11. 62.	*quòd meis omnibus litteris (a. 11. 62. a.) perſtrictus eſſet.*

which

[which were made] in praife of *Pompeius*,	a. 1. 11.62.a	*in Pompeiana laude*,
This day made me a great friend to *Craffus*;	a. 1. 11.63.	*Hic dies me valdè Craffo adiunx:t*;
and yet,	a. 1. 11.64.	*& tamen*,
whatfoeuer came from him openly, or in fecret, was welcome to me.	a. 1. 11.65.	*ab illo apertè, tectè, quicquid eft datum, libenter accepi.*
But I my felfe,	a. 1. 11.66.	*Ego autem ipfe*,
good Gods,	a. 1. 11.67.	*Dÿ boni*,
how well did I behaue mee,	a. 1. 11.68.	*quomodo* **iπιτριπτικευασάμλυ*,
in fauour of my new auditour *Pompeius*?	a. 1. 11.69.	*nouo auditori* Pompeio?
If euer I did abound in arguments.	a. 1. 11.70.	*Si vnquam mihi* **iπιχειρήματα fuppeditauerunt.*
[it was] at that time.	a. 1. 10.71.	*illo tempore.*
what fhould I fay more?	a. 1. 11.72.	*Quid multa?*
there was fhowting.	a. 1. 11.73.	*clamores.*

* Oftentaui me.

* argumenta.

For,

For,	a. 1.	11.74.	*etenim,*
this was the matter [of my difcourfe,]	a. 1.	11.75.	*hæc erat* [x] *ἀπόϑεσις,*
of the Grauitie of the Senate,	a. 1.	11.76.	*de grauitate ordinis,*
of the concord of the Knights,	a. 1.	11.77.	*de equeſtri concordia,*
of the confenting of all *Italy,*	a. 1.	11.78.	*de conſenſio ne* Italiæ,
of the ſpent reliques of the confpiracy,	a. 1.	11.79.	*de immortuis reliquijs coniurationis,*
of the profit,	a. 1.	11.80.	*de vtilitate,*
of the quietneſſe.	a. 1.	11.81.	*de otio.*
You already know what noyſes wee make,	a. 1.	11.82.	*noſti iam (a. 1. 11. 82. a.) ſonitus noſtros,*
vpon ſuch an occaſion,	a. 1.	11.82.a	*in hac materia,*
they were ſo great,	a. 1.	11.83.	*tanti fuerunt,*
that I am the ſhorter,	a. 1.	11.84.	*vt ego eò breuior ſim,*
becauſe I thinke they were heard.	a. 1.	11.85.	*quod eos*(a.1.11.85.a.) *exauditos putem.*

[x] *materia.*

euen

euen from hence	a. 1. 11.85.a	*vſque hinc*
Now the buſineſſe of Rome ſtands thus.	a. 1. 11.86.	*Romanæ autem ſe res ſic habent.*
The Senate [is like that of] *Ariopagus :*	a. 1. 11.87.	*Senatus,* ✱ἄρειⓄ πάγ Ⓞ : ✱Ariopagus.
nothing more conſtant,	a. 1. 11.88.	*nihil conſtantius,*
nothing more ſeuere,	a. 1. 11.89.	*nihil ſeuerius,*
nothing ſtouter.	a. 1. 11.90.	*nihil fortius.*
For,	a. 1. 11.91.	*Nam,*
the day beeing come that the Law ſhould be propounded,	a. 1. 11.92.	*cùm dies veniſſet rogationi* (a.111.92.a) *ferendæ,*
according to the Senats order,	a. 1. 11.92.a	*ex* ✱*S.* ✱*C.* ✱Senatus ✱Conſulto.
the young men of the firſt haire ranne heere & there together,	a. 1. 11.93.	*concurſabant barbatuli iuuenes,*
all that flocke of *Catiline,*	a.1 11.94.	*totus ille grex* Catilinæ,
the young daughter of *Curio* being their guide :	a. 1. 11.95.	*duce filiola* Curionis :
		and

and	a. 1. 11.96.	*&*
they befought the people,	a. 1. 11.97.	*Populum,* (a. 1. 11. 97.a.) *rogabant,*
that they would not admit of the Law,	a. 1. 11.97.a	*vt antiquaret,*
And *Pifo* the Conful,	a. 1. 11.98.	Pifo *autem conful,*
which gaue the law,	a. 1. 11.99.	*lator rogationis,*
was himfelfe a difswader.	a. 1. 11.110.	*idem erat diffuafor.*
Thofe that were made for *Clodius* poffeff'd the bridges,	a. 1. 11.101.	*Operæ Clodianæ ponteis occuparant,*
The tables [wherein the people wrote their voyces] were giuen,	a. 1. 11.102.	*tabella miniftrabantur,*
fo,	a. 1. 11.103.	*ita,*
that there was neuer a placet giuen, [or fiat vti petitur]	a. 1. 11.104.	*vt nulla daretur,* vti Rogas.
Here *Cato* flies, ye to the Roftra or pleading place,	a. 1. 11.105.	*Hic tibi Roftra* Cato *aduolat,*

and

and giues *Piſo* the Conſul very ſhrewd language or reproch:	a. 1.	11.106.	*conuicium* Piſoni *Conſuli mirificum facit :*
if this be reproch,	a. 1.	11.107	*ſi ideſt conuicium,*
[to ſpeake with] a voice, full of grauity, full of authority, and in fine, full of ſafety.	a. 1.	11.108.	*vox plena grauitatis, plena auctoritatis, plena denique ſalutis.*
Thither goes alſo our *Hortenſius,*	a. 1.	11.109.	*Accedit côdem etiam noſter* Hortenſius,
and many good men beſides.	a. 1.	11.110.	*multi praterea boni.*
But *Fauonius* bare himſelfe exceeding well.	a. 1.	11.111.	*Inſignis verò opera* Fauonij *fuit.*
the aſſemblies brake off [or were diſſolued:]	a. 1.	11.112.	*(a.1.11.112. a.) comitia dimittuntur:*
by this concourſe of the beſt of the City	a. 1.	10.112.	*hoc concurſu optima tum*
the Senate was called.	a. 1.	11.113.	*Senatus vocatur.*
when it was decree'd	a. 1.	11.114·	*cùm decerneretur*

in a full Senate,	a. 1.	11.115.	*frequenti Senatu,*
Piso ſtriuing againſt it,	a. 1.	11.116.	*contrà pugnante Pi-ſone,*
[and *Clodius* bow-ing at euery mans feete in particular,	a. 1.	10.117.	*ad pedes omnium ſingillatim accidente* Clodio,
that the conſuls ſhould exhort the people	a. 1.	11.118.	*vt Conſules populum cohortarentur*
to accept of the Law [or Sentence]	a. 1.	11.119.	*ad rogationem accipi-endam,*
about ſome fif-teene men ſecon-ded the opinion of *Curio,* who nullifi-ed the decree of the Senate.	a. 1.	11.120.	*homines ad* *xv.*Cu-rioni, *nullum Senatuſ-conſultum facienti, aſ-ſenſerunt.*
Happily	a. 1.	11.121.	*Facilè*
on the other ſide there were foure hundred.	a. 1.	11.122.	*ex altera parte**cccc. *affuerunt.*
The buſineſſe was diſpatched.	a. 1.	11.123.	*acta res eſt.*
Fuſius granted the third,	a. 1.	11.124.	Fuſius *tertiùm con-ceſsit,*
Clodius made poore ſpeeches :	a. 1.	11.125.	Clodius *contiones miſeras habebat:*
wherein	a. 1.	11.126.	*in quibus*

* quindeci
*patri

*quadring

he

he reprochfully in-iuried *Lucullus, Hortenſius, Caius Piſo,* and *Meſalla* the Conſull :	a. I.	11.127.	Lucullum, Hortenſium, * C. Piſonem, Meſſallam *Conſulem contumelioſè lædebat*:
hee accuſed mee onely for hauing found out all things.	a. I.	11.128.	*me tantùm comperiſſe omnia criminabatur.*
The Senate de-creede,	a. I.	11.129.	*Senatus* (a. I. 11. 129. a. b. c. d. e. f.) *decernebat,*
both	a. I.	11.129.a	*&*
of the Prouinces of the Prætors,	a. I.	11.129.b	*de Prouincijs Prætorum,*
and	a. I.	11.1290.c	*&*
of the legations	a. I.	11.129.d	*de legationibus,*
and	a. I.	11.129.e	*&*
of other matters,	a. I.	11.129. f	*de cæteris rebus,*
that nothing ſhould be done,	a. I.	10.130.	*vt* (a. I. 11. 130. a.) *nequid ageretur ,*
before the Law had beene giuen.	a. I.	11.130.a	*antequàm rogatio lata eſſet.*
You haue vnder-ſtood the affaires of Rome :	a. I.	11.131.	*Habes res Romanas :*
But yet	a. I.	11.132.	*Sed tamen*
heare this alſo,	a. I.	11.133.	*etiam illud* (a. I. 11. 133. a.) *audi,*

* Caium.

which

which I did not looke for,	a. 1.	11.133.a	*quod ego non speraram,*
Mesalla the Consull is an excellent man, ſtout, conſtant, diligent,	a. 1.	11.134	*Meſſalla conſul eſt egregius, fortis, conſtans, diligens,*
a commender, louer, and imitatour of vs.	a. 1.	11.135.	*noſtri laudator, amator, imitator.*
That other	a. 1.	11.136.	*Ille alter,*
[is] leſſe vicious by reaſon of one vice that he hath,	a. 1.	11.137.	*vno vitio minùs vitioſus,*
in that hee is ſlothfull,	a. 1.	11.138.	*quòd iners,*
in that he is drowſie,	a. 1.	11.139.	*quòd ſomni plenus,*
in that he is ignorant,	a. 1.	11.140.	*quòd imperitus,*
in that hee is vnfit for buſineſſe,	a. 1.	11.141.	*quòd * ἀπρακτότατος,*
But	a. 1.	11.142.	*Sed*
he is of ſo wicked a minde through the habit of vice,	a. 1.	11.143.	*voluntate ita *κακίστης,*
that he hath begunne to hate *Pompeius,*	a. 1.	11.144.	*vt Pompeium (a.1. 11.144.a.b.c.) odiſſe cæperit,*
ſince that ſpeech	a. 1.	11.144a	*poſt illam contionem where-*

* rebus agendis ineptus.

* malenolus

wherein	a. 1.	11.144.b	*in qua*
he prayſed the Senate,	a. 1.	11.144.c	*ab eo ſenatus laudatus eſt,*
Therefore	a. 1.	11.145.	*Itaque*
after a ſtrange manner	a. 1.	11.146.	*mirum in modum*
he alienated all good men from him :	a. 1.	11.147.	*omneis à ſe bonos alienauit :*
Neyther did hee this,	a. 1.	11.148.	*neque id (* a. 1. 11. 148.a. *) fecit,*
rather led by the friendſhip of *Clodius;*	a. 1.	10.148.a	*magis amicitia* Clodij *adductus;*
then	a. 1.	11.149.	*quàm*
through an inclination hee hath to deſperate proceedings and factions.	a. 1.	11.149.a	*ſtudio perditarum rerum, atque partium.*
But	a. 1.	11.150.	*Sed*
he hath no man like him	a. 1.	11.151.	*habet ſui ſimilem (* a. 1. 11. 151.a.b. *) neminem*
amongſt the Magiſtrates,	a. 1.	10.151.a	*in magiſtratibus,*
vnleſſe it bee *Fuſius.*	a. 1.	11.151.b	*præter* Fuſium.

Wee

Wee haue good Tribunes of the people, but *Cornutus* [is fo good that hee feemes] another *Cato*.	a. 1.	11.152.	*Bonis vtimur Tribunis* * *pl.* Cornuto *verò Pſeudocatone.*	* Plebis.
What look'ſt thou for?	a. 1.	11.153.	*Quid quæris?*	
that I ſhould now returne to priuate buſineſſes.	a. 1.	11.154.	*nunc vt ad priuata redeam.*	
Teucer hath performed his promiſe.	a. 1.	11.155.	* *πῦμ⊙ promiſſa patrauit.*	* Teucer
Diſpatch thou thoſe things,	a. 1.	11.156.	*Tu mandata effice,*	
which thou haſt vndertaken,	a. 1.	11.157.	*quæ recepiſti,*	
my brother *Quintus* feekes to fell *Tuſculanum,*	a. 1.	11.158.	* *2. frater* (a.1. 11. 158. a.) Tuſculanum *venditat,*	* Quintus
who hath bought the other three parts of the Argiletan houſe for 725. Seſtertij,	a. 1.	11.158.a	*qui Argiletani ædificij reliquum dodrantem emit,* * **HS.** * D C C X X V.	* Seſterti: * Septingenti viginti quinque.
that hee might purchaſe the Pacilian houſe,	a. 1.	11.159.	*vt* (a.1. 11. 159. a.) *emat Pacilianam domum,*	
if he were able.	a. 1.	11.159.a	*ſi poſſit.*	

be

be reconciled with Lucceius.	a. 1. 11.160.	Cum Lucceio in gratiam redi.
I will see the man,	a. 1. 11.161.	Videro hominem,
ther's great suite made :	a. 1. 11. 162	valdè petitur :
I will againe doe mine endeauour,	a. 1. 11.163.	renauabo operam,
Let me heare from thee,	a. 1. 11.164.	Tu (a. 1. 11. 157. a. b.c.)fac me(a. 1. 11. 157. d.)certiorem,
what thou doest,	a. 1. 11.164.a	quid agas,
where thou art,	a. 1. 11.164.b	vbi sis,
how those businesses goe.	a. 1. 11.164.c	cuiusmodi ista res sint.
most diligently	a. 1. 11.164.d	quàm diligentißimè
On the Ides of February,	a. 1. 11.165.	* Idib. * Feb.
Farewell.	a. 1. 11.166.	Vale.
Thou hast heard that Asia is falne to my most sweet brother Quintus:	a. 1. 12. 1.	Asiam Quincto, suauißimo fratri, obtigisse audisti:

* Idibus
* Februarij.

for

for	a. I./I 2. 2.	(a.I.12.2.a.)*enim*
I doubt not,	a. I. I 2.2. a	*non* (a.I.12.2.) *dubito,*
but report will sooner relate this vnto you then any of our letters.	a. I. I 2. 3.	*quin celerius tibi hoc rumor, quàm vllius nostrùm litteræ nuntiarint.*
Now,	a. I. I 2. 4.	*Nunc,*
becaufe wee haue beene alwaies both moft defirous of praife,	a I. I 2. 5.	*quoniam & laudis auidiſſimi ſemper fuimus,*
and	a. I. I 2. 6.	*&*
wee are, and are efteemed more inclined to the *Grecians,*	a. I. I 2. 7.	* (a. I. 12. 7 .a.) φιλίλλημε *& ſumus, & habemur,*
then other men,	a. I. I 2.7. a	*præter cæteros,*
and	a. I. I2. 8.	*&*
we haue vndergone the hatreds, and enmities of many:	a. I. I 2. 9.	*multorum odia, atque inimicitias (a. I. 12. 9.a.) fuſcepimus:*
for the common wealths fake	a. I. I2.9. a	*reipublicæ cauſa*
call to minde the multiplicity of vertue :	a. I. I 2.I 0.	* παντοίης ἀρετῆ ε μιμνήσκεο.

* Græcorum ftudiofi & amatores.

* omnifariæ virtutis reminifcere.

and

and · endeauour with diligence and effect,	a. 1. 12.11.	*curáque & effice,*
that wee may be cōmended, and beloued	a. 1.12.12.	*vt* (a. 1.12. 12.a.) *& laudemur, & amemur*
of all men.	a. 1.11. 12.a	*ab omnibus.*
I will write more vnto thee concerning these matters,	a. 1. 12.13.	*His de rebus plura ad te* (a. 1. 12. 13. a.) *scribam,*
in that epistle	a. 1.12. 13. a	*in ea epistola*
which I will giue to *Quintus* himselfe.	a. 1. 12.14.	*quam ipsi* Quincto *dabo.*
I desire you would let me vnderstand,	a. 1. 12.15.	*Tu me velim certiorem facias,*
what you haue done:	a. 1. 12.16.	*quid* (a. 1.12. 16.a.) *egeris :*
about the affaires that I gaue you in charge,	a. 1. 12.16.a	*de meis mandatis,*
and also	a. 1. 12.17.	*atque etiam,*
what about your owne businesse.	a. 1. 12.18.	* *quid de tuo negotio.* sc: egeris

for

For	a. 1.	12.19.	*Nam*
from the time thou wen'tſt from *Brundiſium*,	a. 1.	12.20.	*vt* Brundiſio *profeⱶus es,*
I haue receiued no letters	a. 1.	12.21.	*nullæ mihi (a. 1. 12. 21.a.)ſunt redditæ litteræ*
from thee.	a. 1.	12.21.a	*abs te.*
I much deſire to know,	a. 1.	12.22.	*Valdè aueo ſcire,*
what you doe.	a. 1.	12.23.	*quid agas.*
On the Ides of March.	a. 1.	12.24.	** Idib. * Mart.*
Farewell.	a. 1.	12.25.	*Vale.*
Thou demandeſt of me,	a. 1.	13. 1.	*Quæris ex me,*
what fell out	a. 1.	13 .2.	*quid acciderit*
about the iudgement,	a. 1.	13.2.a	*de iudicio,*
that it was made ſo different from that which all men expeⱶed,	a. 1.	13. 3.	*quod tam præter opinionem omnium faⱶum ſit,*
and	a. 1.	13. 4.	*&*
	a. 1.	13. 5.	
withall			*ſimul*

* Idibus
* Martij.

thou

thou wilt know,	a. 1.	13. 6.	*vis scire,*
how it comes to passe that I haue combated lesse,	a. 1.	13. 7.	*quomodo ego minus* (a. 1.13.7.a.) *prælia-tus sim,*
then I was wont.	a. 1.	13. 7.a	*quam soleam.*
I will answere thee	a. 1.	13. 8.	*Respondebo tibi.*
preposteroufly, after the manner of *Homer* :	a. 1.	13. 9.	* ὕστερον πρότερον ὁμηρικῶς ;
for I,	a. 1.	13..10	*ego enim,*
as long as the authority of the Senate was to bee defended by mee,	a. 1.	13.11.	*quamdiu Senatus authoritas mihi defendenda fuit,*
I fought so eagerly and earneftly,	a. 1.	13.12.	*sic acriter & vehementer præliatus sum,*
that a clamour, and concourse were made	a. 1.	13.13.	*vt clamor concursús-que* (a. 1. 13.13.a.) *fierent*
with my great cōmendation :	a. 1.	13.13.a	*maxima cum mea laude :*
but if I haue seemed to thee to haue beene ftout at any time	a. 1.	13.14.	*quòd si tibi vnquam sum visus* (a. 1. 13. 14.a.) *fortis.*
in the Commonwealth,	a. 1.	13.14. a	*in * rep.*
verily	a. 1.	13.14 b	*certè*

*Ordine conuerso Homericè.

* republica.

thou

thou wouldſt haue admired me	a. 1.	13.15.	*me* (a.1. 13. 15. a.) *admiratus eſſes*
in that cauſe :	a. 1.	13.15.a	*in illa cauſa :*
for	a. 1.	13.16.	(a.1.13.16.a.) *enim*
when as he had re-courſe to . making ſpeeches to the peo-ple,	a. 1.	13.16.a	*cùm* (a.1. 13. 16.) **ille ad conciones con-fugiſſet,*
and in them	a. 1.	13.17.	*in ijſque*
vſed my name to breede hatred,	a. 1.	13. 18.	*meo nomine ad inui-diam vteretur,*
Good gods,	a. 1.	13.19.	*Dij immortales,*
what battayles, & how bloody con-flicts produced I?	a. 1.	14.20.	*quas ego pugnas, & quantas ſtrages edi-di ?*
what aſſaults made I againſt *Piſo, Curio,* and againſt all that companie?	a. 1.	13.21.	*Quos impetus in* Pi-ſonē, *in* Curionem, *in totam illam manum feci ?*
how did I perſe-cute the leuitie of the old men, and the lycenciouſneſſe of the young ?	a. 1.	13.22.	*quomodo ſum inſecta-tus leuitatem ſenum, libidinem iuuentutis ?*
often,	a. 1.	13.23.	*ſæpè,*
as the Gods ſhall helpe me,	a.1.	13.24.	*ita me dij iuuent,*

* Clodius

I

I did not onely defire thy prefence to counfell me, but alfo to be a fpecta-tour of myne admirable encounters.	a. 1. 13.25.	te non folùm aucto-rem confiliorum meo-rum , verùm etiam fpectatorem pugnarum mirificarum defidera-ui.
But after *Hortenfius* thought,	a. 1. 13.26.	Poftea verò quàm Hortenfius excogita-uit,
that *Fufius* Tribune of the people fhould giue the Lawe,	a. 1. 13.27.	ut legem (a. 1. 13. 27.a.) Fufius *Tribunus plebis ferret,*
concerning the religion	a. 1. 13.27.a	de religione
in which	a. 1. 13.28.	in qua
it differed nothing	a. 1. 13.29.	nihil aliud (a. 1. 13. 29.a.) differebat
from the confular Law,	a. 1. 13.29.a	à confulari rogatione,
but in the quality of the Iudges:	a. 1. 13.30.	nifi Iudicum genus ;
(for all confifted therein)	a. 1. 13.31.	(in eo autem erant omnia)
and	a. 1. 12.32.	(a. 1. 13.32.a.) que.
he vfed all his power	a. 1. 13.32.a	pugnauit
that it might bee fo,	a. 1. 13.33.	vt ita fieret,

be-

becauſe hee had perſwaded himſelfe and others,	a. 1.	13.34.	quòd & ſibi, & alijs perſuaſerat,
that hee could not eſcape [puniſhment] whoſoeuer were his Iudges:	a. 1.	13.35.	nullis illum Iudicibus effugere poſſe:
I puld downe my ſayles,	a. 1.	13.36.	contraxi vela,
perceiuing the want of Iudges:	a. 1.	13.37.	perſpiciens inopiam Iudicum:
neyther gaue I any teſtimony,	a. 1.	13.38.	neque dixi quidquam pro teſtimonio,
but	a. 1.	13.39.	niſi
that which was ſo known and teſtified,	a. 1.	13.40.	quod erat ita notum, teſtatum,
that I could not omit to ſpeake thereof.	a. 1.	13.41.	vt non poſſem præterire.
Therefore,	a. 1.	13.42.	Itaque,
if thou deſireſt to know the cauſe of the abſolution,	a. 1.	13.43.	ſi cauſam quæris abſolutionis,
To turne to that that I firſt propoſed,	a. 1.	13.44.	vt iam * πρὸς τὸ ϖρότερϑ reuertar,

ˣ ad prius.

it

It was the pouerty, and corruption of the Iudges.	a. 1. 13.46.	*egestas Iudicum fuit, & turpitudo.*
And that this happened, the opinion of *Hortensius* was the occasion :	a. 1. 13 47.	*Id autem vt accideret, commissum est Hortensij consilio :*
who	a. 1. 13.48.	*qui*
doubting,	a. 1. 13.49.	*dum veritus est,*
left *Fusius* should oppose that law,	a. 1. 13.50.	*ne Fusius ei legi intercederet,*
which was exhibited,	a. 1. 13.51.	*quæ* (a.1.13.51.a.) *ferebatur.*
by order of the Senate	a. 1. 13.51.a	*ex * S. * C.*
he perceyued not	a. 1. 13.52.	*non vidit*
that it was more fitting,	a. 1. 13.53.	*illud satius esse,*
that he should liue in infamie and basenesse,	a. 1. 13.54.	*illum in infamia relinqui, ac sordibus,*
then	a. 1. 13.55.	*quàm*
be committed to vniust iudgement.	a. 1. 13.56.	*infirmo iudicio committi.*

* Senatus
* Consulto.

But

But,	a. 1.	13.57.	*Sed,*
led with hatred,	a. 1.	13.58.	*ductus odio,*
hee haftened to bring the bufineffe to an hearing,	a. 1.	13.59.	*properauit rem deducere in iudicium,*
though he fayde	a. 1.	13.60.	*cùm* (a.1.13.60.a.) *tamen diceret*
notwithftanding the fword were of lead he would haue his throate cut.	a. 1.	13.60. a	*illum plumbeo gladio iugulatum iri.*
But	a. 1.	13.61.	*Sed*
if you feeke to know,	a. 1.	13.62.	(a. 1. 13. 62. a.) *ſi quæris,*
what the iudgement was :	a. 1.	13.62.a	*Iudicium quale fuerit :*
· the iffue thereof was incredible :	a. 1.	13.63.	*incredibili exitu :*
So as now, vpon the euent by others,	a. 1.	13.64.	*ſic vti nunc ex euentu ab alijs,*
yet by mee from the very beginning the councell of *Hortenſius* was reprehended.	a. 1.	13.65.	*à me tamen ex ipſo initio conſilium Hortenſij reprehendatur.*
For,	a. 1.	13.66.	*Nam,*

the

the Iudges being refuted	a. 1. 13.67.	*vt reiectio facta est*
with exceeding great outcryes,	a. 1. 13. 67.a	*clamoribus maximis,*
when as the accuser reiected the wickedest,	a. 1. 13. 68.	*cum accusator (a. 1. 13. 68. a.) homines nequißimos reijceret,*
as a good Cen-sor,	a. 1. 13. 68.a	*tanquam Censor bonus,*
and the defendant, putting apart euery one that was most frugall :	a. 1. 13.69.	*reus, (a.1.13.69.a.) frugalißimum quemque secerneret :*
as a mercifull Fencemaster,	a. 1. 13.69.a	*tanquam clemens lanista,*
as soone as the Iudges were set,	a. 1. 13.70.	*vt primùm Iudices consederunt,*
the good men be-gan greatly to di-strust :	a. 1. 13.71.	*valdè diffidere boni cœperunt :*
for	a. 1. 13.72.	*(a.1.13.72.a.) enim*
there neuer met a more base compa-nie	a. 1. 13.72.a	*non(a.1.13.72.)vnquam turpior (a.1.13.72.b.) confeßus fuit :*
in a dicing house:	a. 1. 13.72.b	*in ludo talario :*

Stay-

Stayned Sena-tours,	a. 1.	13.73.	*maculosi Senatores,*
bare Knights,	a. 1.	13.74.	*nudi equites,*
Tribunes lesse sto-red with treasure then with name of treasurers.	a. 1.	13.75.	*Tribuni non tam æra-ti,quàm,vt appellantur ærarii.*
Yet	a. 1.	13.76.	(a. 1. 13. 36. a.) *Tamen*
there were some few good men a-mongst them.	a. 1.	13.76.a	*pauci* (a.1.13.76.) *boni inerant,*
which hee could not put off when hee refuted the rest:	a. 1.	13.77.	*quos reiectione fugare ille non potucrat:*
who sate sad and heauily,	a. 1.	13.78.	*qui mæsti* (a.1.13.78. a.) *& mærētes sedebāt.*
amongst such as were vnlike vnto them,	a. 1.	13.78.a	*inter sui dissimileis,*
and	a. 1.	13.79.	*&*
were vehemently moued	a. 1.	13.80.	(a. 1.13.80.a.) *vehe-mentor permonebātur*
with the contagi-on of basenesse.	a. 1.	13.80.a	*contagione turpitu-dinis.*
Heere,	a. 1.	13.81.	*Hîc,*

eue-

euery businesse as it was referred to the Councell,	a. 1.	13.82.	*vt quæque res ad consilium* (a. 1. 13.82. a.)*referebatur,*
vpon the first demaunds	a. 1.	13.82.a	*primis postulationibus*
was an incredible seueritie,	a. 1.	13.83.	*incredibilis erat seueritas,*
without any variety of opinion.	a. 1.	13.84.	*nulla varietate sententiarum.*
the defendant could intreate no fauour;	a. 1.	13.85.	*nihil impetrabat reus;*
more was granted to the playntife,	a.1.	13.86.	*plus accusatori dabatur,*
then he desired.	a. 1.	13.87.	*quàm postulabat.*
Hortensius triumphed.	a. 1.	13.88.	*triumphabat* (a.1. 13.88.a.)*Hortēsius.*
what would you more?	a. 1.	13.88.a	*quid quæris?*
that he had [fore] seene so much.	a. 1.	13.89.	*se vidisse tantum.*
There was no man,	a. 1.	13.90.	*Nemo erat,*
which thought him not guilty, and a thousand tymes condemned:	a. 1.	13.91.	*qui illium reum, ac non millies condemnatum arbitraretur:*

but|

but I being pro-duced as a wit-neſſe,	a. 1.	13.92.	*me verò teſte produ-cto,*
I preſume that you haue vnder-ſtood	a. 1.	13.93.	*credo te* (a. i. 13. 93.a.) *audîſſe*
by the cry of *Clo-dius* friends,	a. 1.	13.93.a	*ex acclamatione* Clo-dij *aduocatorum,*
what a riſing was made of the Iudg-es,	a. 1.	13.94.	*quæ conſurrectio Iu-dicum facta ſit,*
how they came a-about me,	a. 1.	13.95.	*vt me circumſtete-rint,*
how they made ſhew vnto *Clodius* manifeſtly that they were ready to lay downe their liues.	a. 1.	13.96.	*vt apertè ingula ſua* (a.1.13.96.a.) * P. Clodio *oſtentarint.*
for my ſafety :	a. 1.	13.96. a	*pro meo capite :*
which ſeemed much more honou-rable to me,	a. 1.	13.97.	*quæ mihi res multò honorificentior viſa eſt,*
then	a. 1.	13.98.	*quàm*
eyther that,	a. 1.	13.99.	*aut illa,*
when your Citi-zens forbad *Xeno-crates* to giue teſti-mony by oath,	a. 1.	13.100.	*cùm iurare tui ciues* Xenocratem , *teſti-monium dicentem,pro-hibuerunt,*

* Publio,

or

or	a. I.	13.101.	*aut*
when our Iudges would not behold the tables of *Metellus Numidicus*,	a. I.	13.102.	*cùm tabulas* Metelli Numidici (a. I. 13. 102. a.) *noſtri Iudices aſpicere noluerunt,*
when they were carried about,	a. I.	13.102.a	*cùm hæ (a. I. 13. 102.b.) circumferrentur,*
(as the cuſtome is:)	a. I.	13.102.b	*(vt mos eſt:)*
I ſay	a. I.	13.103.	*(a. I. 13.103.a.) inquam*
this buſineſſe of ours is much greater:	a. I.	14. 103.a	*multò hæc (a. I. 13. 103.) noſtra res maior.*
Therefore	a. I.	13.104.	*Itaque*
the defendant being caſt by the voyce of the Iudges,	a. I.	13.105.	*Iudicum vocibus (a. I. 13.105.a.) fractus reus,*
(ſeeing I was defended by them ſo)	a. I.	13.105. a	*(cùm ego ſic ab his (a. I. 13.105.b.) defenderer)*
as if I had beene the ſafety of [my] countrie	a. I.	13.105.b	*vt ſalus patriæ*
and herewithall	a. I.	13.106.	*& unà*

all

all that ftood in his defence fell from him.	a. 1. 13.107.	*patroni omnes conciderunt.*
on the other fide	a. 1. 13.108.	a.**1.13.108.**a.) *autem*
the fame concourfe thronged to mee the day following,	a. 1. 13.108.a	*ad me*(a.**1.13.108.**) *eadem frequentia poftridie conuenit,*
by which I was accompanied to my houfe.	a. 1. 13.109.	*quacum* (a. 1. 13. 109. a.) *fum domum reductus.*
leauing the Confulfhip,	a. 1. 13.109.a	*abiens confulatu,*
the excellent Ariopagite cryed out,	a. 1. 13.110.	*clamare præclari Ariopagitæ,*
that they would not come,	a. 1. 13.111.	*fe non effe uenturos,*
vnleffe a guard were appoynted them.	a. 1. 13.112.	*nifi præfidio conftituto.*
It was referred to the Councell.	a. 1. 13.113.	*refertur ad confilium.*
one opinion and no more approoued not that there fhuld bee a guard appointed.	a. 1. 13.114.	*vna fola fententia præfidium non defiderauit.*

The

The matter was brought vnto the Senate,	a. 1. 13.115.	*Defertur res ad Senatum,*	
It was moſt grauely and worthily determined,	a. 1. 13.116.	*grauiſsimè, ornatiſsiméque decernitur.*	
The Iudges are commended.	a. 1. 13.117.	*Laudantur Iudices.*	
The buſineſſe is giuen to the Magiſtrates :	a. 1. 13.118.	*Datur negotium magiſtratibus :*	
no man thought the man would anſwere for himſelfe.	a. 1. 13.119.	*reſponſurũ hominem nemo arbitrabatur.*	
Now tell me, *Muſes,*	a. 1. 13.120.	* ἔσπετε νῦ μοι μοῦσαι,	* dicite nunc mihi, Muſæ.
how this fire firſt fell.	a. 1. 13.121.	*Ὅππως δὴ πρῶτον πῦρ ἔμπεσον.	*quomodo primò ignis incidit.
Thou knoweſt *Caluus,* he of the *Nanneiani,*	a. 1. 13.122.	*Noſti* Caluum *ex* Nanneianis, *illum,*	
that commender of mee :	a. 1. 13.123.	*illum laudatorem meum :*	
of whoſe Oration made to my honour I wrote vnto you.	a. 1. 13.124.	*de cuius Oratione erga me honorifica ad te ſcripſeram.*	

In

In the fpace of two dayes	a. 1.	13.125.	*biduo*
by one feruant,	a. 1.	13.126.	*per vnum feruum,*
and that of the company of Fencers,	a. 1.	13.127.	*& eum ex gladiatorio ludo,*
he ended all the bufineffe :	a. 1.	13.128.	*confecit totum negotium :*
hee called vnto him,	a. 1.	13.129.	*accerſiuit ad ſe,*
he promifed,	a. 1.	13.130.	*promiſit,*
hee gaue fecurity,	a. 1.	13.131.	*intercesſit,*
he gaue [ready money.]	a. 1.	13.132.	*dedit.*
But now,	a. 1.	13.133.	*Iam verò,*
O good gods,	a. 1.	13.134.	*O dij boni,*
what mifchiefe !	a. 1.	13.135.	*rem perditam!*
euen	a. 1.	13.136.	*etiam*
the nights of certaine women,	a. 1.	13.137.	*noctes certarum mulierum,*
and	a. 1.	13.138.	*atque*
the introductions of young Gentlemen,	a. 1.	13.139.	*adoleſcentulorum nobilium introductiones,*

to some Iudges	a. 1.	13.140.	*nonnullis Iudicibus,*
were in stead of full payment.	a. 1.	13. 141.	*pro mercedis cumulo fuerunt.*
So that	a. 1.	13.142.	*Ita*
by a notable departure of the good men,	a. 1.	13.143.	*summo discessu bonorum,*
by a full forum of seruants,	a. 1.	13.144.	*pleno foro seruorum,*
twenty Iudges were notwithstanding so stout,	a. 1.	13.145.	*＊xx. Iudices ita fortes tamen fuerunt,*
that,	a. 1.	13.146.	*vt,*
in exceeding great danger,	a. 1.	13.147.	*summo proposito periculo,*
they chose rather to perish,	a. 1.	13.148.	*vel perire maluerint,*
then	a. 1.	13.149.	*quàm*
to destroy all things.		13.150.	*perdere omnia.*
There were thirty,	a. 1.	13.151.	*＊xxx. fuerunt,*
whom famine will moue rather then fame.	a. 1.	13.152.	*quos fames magis, quàm fama commouerit.*

＊ Viginti.

＊ Triginta.

Of

Of whom, when *Catulus* had feene one,	a. 1.	13.153.	*Quorum* Catulus *cùm vidiſſet quendam,*
hee ſayd,	a. 1.	13.154.	(a.1.13.154.a.) *inquit,*
Why did you demand a guard?	a. 1.	13.154.a	*Quid vos,* (a. 1.13. 154.) *præſidium vobis poſtulabatis?*
did you feare,	a. 1.	13.155.	*an* (a. 113. 155.a.) *timebatis,*
your money ſhould bee taken from you?	a. 1.	13.155.a	*ne nummi vobis eriperentur?*
you haue heard the manner of the iudgement, and the cauſe of the abſolution,	a. 1.	13.156.	*habes* (a.1.13.156.a.) *genus iudicij, & cauſam abſolutionis,*
as briefely as I could.	a. 1.	13.156.a	*vt breuiſſimè potui.*
You demand further,	a. 1.	13.157.	*Quæris deinceps,*
in what ſtate the Common Wealth and I now ſtand.	a. 1.	13.158.	*quis nunc ſit ſtatus * reipub. & qui meus.*

* reipublicæ

You

You shall know that that state of the Commonwealth is falne out of our hands,	a. 1. 13. 159.	Reipublicæ ſtatum illum (a.1. 13.159. a. b.f.) elapſum ſcito eſſe de manibus,
which you thought had been confirmed by my counſell, and I by diuine,	a. 1. 13.159.a	quem tu meo conſilio, ego diuino confirmatum putabam,
which ſeemed to haue bin confirmed and founded,	a. 1. 13.159.b	qui (a.1. 13.159.c. d.e.) fixus & fundatus eſſe videbatur,
by the vnion of all good men,	a. 1. 13.159.c	bonorum omnium coniunctione,
and	a.1. 13.159.d	&
by the authoritie of my Conſulſhip,	a. 1. 13.159.e	auctoritate conſulatus mei,
vnleſſe ſome God doe looke vpon vs,	a. 1. 13.159.f	niſi quis Deus nos reſpexerit,
by this only iudgement :	a. 1. 13.160.	vno hoc iudicio :
if it be a iudgement,	a. 1. 13.161.	ſi iudicium eſt,
that thirtie of the lighteſt and moſt malicious men amongſt the people of Rome, ſhould deſtroy all law and equitie,	a. 1. 13.162.	triginta homines populi * R. leuiſsimos, ac nequiſsimos (a.1.13. 162.a.) ius ac fas omne delere,

* Romani.

for

for a little money,	a. 1. 13. 162. a	*nummulis acceptis,*
and	a. 1. 13.163.	*&*
that which all not only men, but beasts know to haue been done,	a. 1. 13.164.	*quod omnes non modò homines, verùm etiam pecudes factum esse sciebant,*
that *Caluus , Plau- tus,Spongia,* and such like trifling compa- nions,conclude,that the same was neuer done.	a. 1. 13.165.	*id* Caluum, *&* Plautum, *&* Spon- giam, *& cæteras hu- iusmodi quisquilias, statuere, nunquam esse factum.*
But yet,	a.1. 13.166.	*Sed tamen,*
that I may comfort you,	a. 1. 13.167.	*vt te (a.1. 13. 159. a.) consoler,*
about the Com- monwealth,	a. 1. 13.168.	*de* * *rep.*
wickednesse doth not so glory, ioyfull in the victorie,	a. 1. 13.169.	*non ita,(a. 13. 169. a. b.) alacris exsultat improbitas in victoria,*
as bad men hoped,	a. 1. 13.169. a	*vt sperarunt mali,*
with so great a wound giuen to the Commonwealth :	a. 1. 13.169.b	*tanto imposito* * *reip. vulnere :*
for	a. 1. 13.170.	*nam*
they certainely thought as much :	a. 1. 13.171.	*planè ita putauerunt,*

* republic

* reipublic

when

when religion, whē modefty, when the faith of the Iudges, when the Senats authority fhuld faile,	a. 1.	13.172.	*cùm religio, cùm pudicitia, cum Iudiciorum fides, cùm Senatus auctoritas concidiffet,*
that it would come to paffe,	a. 1.	13.173.	*fore,*
that wickedneffe and luft hauing the vpper hand, fhould openly be reuenged of euery good man for the wrong,	a. 1.	13.174.	*vt apertè victrix nequitia, ac libido, pœnas ab optimo quoque peteret fui doloris,*
which the feuerity of my Confulfhip had inflicted vpon euery one that was a moft wicked liuer.	a. 1.	13.175.	*quem improbifsimo cuique inufferat feueritas confulatus mei.*
I the fame man	a. 1.	13.176.	*Idem ego ille*
(for I do not hold my felfe	a. 1.	13.177.	*(non enim mihi videor*
infolently to boaft,	a. 1.	13.178.	*infolenter gloriari,*
when I fpeake with you concerning my felfe,	a. 1.	13.179.	*cùm de me apud te loquor,*
efpecially in that Epiftle,	a. 1.	13.180.	*in ea præfertim epiftola,*

which

which I would not haue to bee read to others,)	a. 1.	13.181.	*quam nolo alijs legi)*
I say,	a. 1.	13.182.	*(a.1.13.182.a.)inquã,*
I the same man re-created the afflicted minds of good men,	a. 1.	13.182.a	*Idem,(a.1.13.182.) ego recreaui affli-ctos animos bonorum,*
confirming, incou-raging, and stirring vp euery one,	a. 1.	13.183.	*vnumquenque confir-mans, & excitans,*
I tooke away also all libertie of spea-king, from corrupt Iudges that were to be prosecuted and reprehended.	a. 1.	13.184.	*insectandis verò, ex-agitandisque numma-rijs Iudicibus, omnem (a. 1. 13. 184. a.) * παῤῥησίαν eripui.*
from all such as sought and fauoured that Victory,	a. 1.	13.184.a	*omnibus studiosis, ac fautoribus illius vi-ctoriæ,*
I neuer suffered the Consul *Piso* to haue his wil in any thing:	a. 1.	13.185.	*Pisonem consulem nulla in re consistere vnquam sum passus:*
I tooke *Syria* from the man to whom it was already promi-sed :	a. 1.	13.186.	*desponsam homini iam Syriam ademi:*
I recalled the Se-nate to their won ted seueritie,	a. 1.	13.187.	*Senatum ad pristinam suam seueritatem re-uocaui,*

* loquendi licentiam.

and

and	a. 1.	13.188.	*atque*
I rayſed it from ſlauery :		13.189.	*abiectum excitaui :*
I confounded *Clodius*, that was preſent in the Senate,	a. 1.	13.190.	Clodium *præſentem fregi in Senatu,*
both	a. 1.	13.191.	*cùm*
with a continued ſpeech,	a. 1.	13.192.	*oratione perpetua,*
[and] very full of grauity,	a. 1.	13.193.	*pleniſsima grauitatis,*
and alſo	a. 1.	13.194.	*tùm*
with a contention of this ſort,	a. 1.	13.195.	*altercatione huiuſmodi,*
whereof I am willing you ſhuld haue ſome taſte.	a. 1.	13.196.	*ex qua licet pauca deguſtes.*
For	a. 1.	13.197.	*Nam*
the reſt can neyther haue the ſame force nor comelineſſe,	a. 1.	13.198.	*cætera non poſſunt habere eandem neque vim, neq; venuſtatem,*
that earneſtneſſe of contention beeing layd apart,	a. 1.	13.199.	*remoto illo ſtudio contentionis,*
which you call A-gona, or the conflict.	a. 1.	13.200.	*quem* * ἀγῶνα *vos appellatis.* ‹* certamen.›

For,

For,	a. 1.	13.201.	*Nam,*
being assembled on the Ides of May,	a. 1.	13.202.	*vt idibus Maÿs (a. 1. 13.202.a.)conuenim⁹,*
in the Senate,	a. 1.	13. 202.a	*in Senatum,*
I being asked mine opinion,	a. 1.	13.203.	*rogatus ego sententiam,*
I spake many things	a. 1.	13.204.	*multa dixi*
about that, that neerely touched the Commonwealth,	a. 1.	13.205.	*de summa * reip.*
and	a. 1.	13.206.	*atque*
that place was by me diuinely broght in,	a. 1.	13.207.	*ille locus inductus à me est diuinitùs,*
That the Conscript Fathers or Senate should not bee dismaied or faint :	a. 1.	13.208.	*Ne,(a. 1.13.208.a.) * P. * C.conciderent, ne deficerent :*
for hauing receiued one stroke,	a. 1.	13.208.a	*vnâ plagâ acceptâ,*
[and] that the wound was such,	a. 1.	13.209.	*vulnus esse eiusmodi,*
that I thought it was neyther to bee dissembled nor feared,	a. 1.	13.210.	*quòd mihi neque dissimulandum , neque pertimescendum videretur,*

*reipublicæ.

* P.Patres.
* C.Conscripti.

lest

left wee mought bee iudged eyther foolifh for being ignorant thereof, or very cowards for being timorous.	a. 1. 13.211.	*ne aut ignorando ftul-tifsimi, aut metuendo ignauifsimi iudicare-mur.*
[And] that *Len-tulus* and *Catiline* were twice abfol-ued:	a. 1. 13.212.	*Bis abfolutum effe* Lentulum, *bis* Catilinam :
[and] that now this third was by the Iudges put vpon the Common-Wealth.	a. 1. 13.213.	*hunc tertium iam effe à Iudicibus in* * *remp. immiffum.*
Thou art deceiued, *Clodius,*	a. 1. 13.214.	*Erras,* Clodi,
the Iudges haue not referued thee for the citty, but for the prifon :	a. 1. 13.215.	*non te Iudices vrbi,fed carceri referuarunt :*
neyther haue they determination to keep thee in towne, but to depriue thee thereof by banifh-ment :	a. 1. 13.216.	*neque retinere in ci-uitate, fed exfilio pri-uare voluerunt :*
wherefore,	a. 1. 13 217.	*Quamobrem,*
O Confcript Fa-thers,	a. 1. 13.218.	**P.** *C.*

* rempubli-cam,

* P.Patres.
* C Con-fcripti.

be

be of good courage,	a. 1. 13. 219.	*erigite animos,*
mayntaine your honour,	a. 1. 13. 220.	*retinete veſtram dignitatem,*
that conſent of good men remayneth in the common wealth :	a. 1. 13. 221.	*manet illa in * rep. bonorum conſenſio :*
griefe is falne vpon good men,	a. 1. 13. 222.	*dolor acceſſit bonis viris,*
[but their] vertue is no whit leſſened.	a. 1. 13. 223.	*virtus non eſt imminuta.*
There is no hourt done that's new :	a. 1. 13. 224.	*Nihil eſt damni faĉtum noui :*
but,	a. 1. 13. 225.	*ſed,*
what was [hidden]	a. 1. 13. 126.	*quod erat,*
is diſcouered in the iudgement of one wicked fellow:	a. 1. 13. 227.	*inuentum eſt in vnius hominis perditi iudicio*
more are found like [to him.]	a. 1. 13. 228.	*plures ſimiles reperti ſunt.*
But	a. 1. 13. 229.	*Sed*
what doe I?	a. 1. 13. 230.	*quid ago ?*
I haue almoſt put an oration in an epiſtle.	a. 1. 13. 231.	*pænè orationem in epiſtolam incluſi.*

* republica

I

I returne to the Controuerfie.	a. 1. 13.232	Redeo ad altercatio-nem.
The faire boy ari-feth,	a. 1. 13.233.	Surgit pulchellus puer,
hee obiecteth to me	a. 1. 13.234.	obijcit mihi
that I was at the Baiæ.	a. 1. 13.235.	me ad Baias fuiſſe.
'Tis falfe,	a. 1. 13.236.	Falfum,
but yet	a. 1. 13.237.	fed tamen
wherein is this like to that,	a. 1. 13.238.	quid huic fimile eſt,
faid I,	a. 1. 13.239.	inquam?
as though you meane I went to hide me?	a. 1. 13.240.	quafi in operto dicas fuiſſe.
What hath a man of Arpinas to doe with hot waters?	a. 1. 13.241.	Quid (a.1.13.241. a.) homini Arpinati cum aquis calidis?
faid he,	a. 1. 13.241.a	inquit,
Tell him that de-fends you,	a. 1. 13.242.	Narra (a.1. 13.242. a.) patrono tuo,
faid I,	a. 1. 13.242.a	inquam,
who defired the waters of Arpinas:	a. 1. 13.243.	qui Arpinateis aquas concupiuit.
for you know the Sea [Waters.]	a. 1. 13.244.	noſti enim Marinas.

How

How long fhall we fuffer this King,	a. i.	13.245.	*Quoufq;* (a. I. 13.245. a) *hunc regē feremus?*
faid he?	a. i.	13. 245. a	*inquit,*
Doeft thou fpeake of a King,	a. i.	13.246.	*Regem appellas,*
faid I,	a. i.	13.247.	*inquam,*
who being King, makeft no mention of thy felfe?	a. i.	13.248.	*cùm Rex tui mentionem nullam feceris?*
for he in hope had fwallowed the inheritance of a kingdome.	a. i.	13.249.	*ille autem Regis hæreditatem ſpe deuorarat.*
Thou haft bought a houfe,	a. i.	13.250.	*Domũ* (a.i. 13.250. a.) *emiſti.*
faid he,	a. i.	13.250. a	*inquit,*
doeft thou meane to fay thou haft bought Iudges?	a. i.	13.251.	*Putas* (a.i. 13.251.a.) *dicere, Iudices emiſti?*
Said I,	a. i.	13.251.a	*Inquam,*
They did not credit thine oath.	a. i.	13.252.	*Iuranti* (a.i.13.252. a.) *tibi non crediderũt.*
Said he,	a. i.	13.252.a	*Inquit,*
But twenty Iudges did credit me.	a. i.	13.253.	*Mihi verò* (a.i.13.253. a.)*xx. indices crediderũt*
Said I,	a. i.	13.253.a	*Inquam,*
Thirty did not giue thee any credit,	a. i.	13.254.	*xxx.* (a.i.13.254.a.) *tibi nihil crediderunt,*

viginti.

triginta.

becaufe

becaufe they re-ceiued money be-forehand.	a. 1.	13.254.a	*quoniam nummos ante acceperunt.*
Troubled with the great clamours,	a. 1.	13.255.	*Magnis clamoribus afflictus,*
he held his peace,	a. 1.	13.256.	*conticuit,*
and	a. 1.	13.257.	*&*
he abated his cou-rage.	a. 1.	13.258.	*concidit.*
But thus ſtand things with vs.	a. 1.	13.259.	*Noſter autem ſtatus eſt hic.*
With thoſe that are good, we are the ſame that you left vs,	a. 1.	13.260.	*apud bonos ijdem ſumus, quos reliquiſti:*
with the ſcumme and dregges of the Citie, much better then you left vs.	a. 1.	13.261.	*apud ſordem vrbis, & fæcem, multò melius quàm reliquiſti.*
For	a. 1.	13.262.	*Nam*
not ſo much as this doth hurt vs,	a. 1.	13.263.	*& illud nobis non obeſt,*
that it ſeemeth not that our teſtimonie was of any value.	a. 1.	13.264.	*videri noſtrum teſtimonium non valuiſſe.*
The bloud of enuy hath beene drawne	a. 1.	13.265.	*Miſſus eſt ſanguis inuidiæ*
without paine:		13.266.	*ſine dolore :*

Yea

Yea and so much the rather,	a. 1.	13.267	*Atque etiam hoc magis,*
that all those fauourers of his wickednesse doe confesse,	a. 1.	13.268.	*quòd omnes illi fautores illius flagitij, (a.1.13.268.a.)confitentur,*
that the businesse was manifestly carried by bribing the Iudges.	a. 1.	13.268.a	*rem manifestam illam redemtam esse à Iudicibus.*
Whereunto may be added,	a. 1.	13.269.	*Accedit illud,*
that, that Parlamentarie leeche of the treasurie, that miserable, and fasting Communaltie thinketh :	a. 1.	13.270.	*quòd illa contionalis hirudo ærarij, misera, & ieiuna plebecula (a.1.13.270.a.) putat:*
that I am entirely beloued of this *Magnus,*		13.270.a	*me ab hoc* Magno *vnicè diligi,*
and	a. 1.	13.271.	*&*
indeede	a. 1.	13.272.	*hercule*
we are vnited together with much and pleasing familiaritie,	a. 1.	13.273.	*multa , & iucunda consuetudine coniuncti inter nos sumus,*
in such sort,	a. 1.	13.274.	*vsque eò,*

that

that thofe our con-forts of the conjuration, little bearded young men, call him in their ordinarie talke *Cneus Cicero.*	a. 1.	13.275.	*vt noſtri iſti comeſſatores coniurationis, barbatuli iuuenes, illum in ſermonibus,* Cn. Ciceronem *appellent.*	ˣ Cneium.
Therefore	a. 1.	13.276.	*Itaque*	
both at the Playes, and at the Prizes we carried away wonderfull ſhewes [of loue and courtefie]	a. 1.	13.277.	*& ludis, & gladiatoribus mirãdas* ˣ ἐπισημασίας (a.1.13.277. a) *auferebamus.*	ˣ Significationes geſtuum.
without the pipe of any ſhepheard.	a. 1.	13. 277 a	*ſine vlla paſtoritia fiſtula.*	
At this prefent	a. 1.	13.278.	*Nunc*	
wee expeẛ the commencements or choofing of Magiſtrates,	a. 1.	13.279.	*eſt expeẛatio comitiorum,*	
into which our *Magnus* thruſts the fonne of *Aulus,*	a. 1.	13.280.	*in qua* (a.1.13.280. a.) *trudit noſter* Magnus Auli ˣ F.	ˣ F.Filium.
in defpite of all men,	a. 1.	13.280.a	*omnibus inuitis,*	
and	a. 1.	13.281.	*atque*	
therein	a. 1.	13.282.	*in eo*	

hee

hee neither vſeth authoritie, nor fauour,	a. 1.	13.283.	*neq; auctoritate, neq; gratia pugnat,*
but	a. 1.	13.284.	*ſed*
ſuch as *Philip* ſaid that all Caſtles were taken withall,	a. 1.	13.285.	*quibus* Philippus *omnia Caſtella expugnari poſſe dicebat,*
ſo that an Aſſe, loaden with gold, might get vp into them.	a. 1.	13.286.	*in quæ modò aſellus, onuſtus auro, poſſet adſcendere.*
And they ſay that Conſull hath vndergone the buſineſſe,	a. 1.	13.287.	*Conſul autem ille (a. 1. 13.287.a.) ſuſcepiſſe negotium dicitur,*
that's likened to the worſt player,	a. 1.	13.287.a	*deterioris hiſtrionis ſimilis,*
and	a. 1.	13.288.	*&*
that he hath thoſe that are to make the diuiſions at home:	a. 1.	13.289.	*domi diuiſores habere:*
which I beleeue not.	a. 1.	13.290.	*quod ego non credo.*
But	a. 1.	13.291.	*Sed*
there are alreadie two Decrees of the Senate made odious,	a. 1.	13.292.	* S. * C. *duo iam facta ſunt odioſa,*

* S, Senatu
* C. Conſul

becauſe

becaufe they are thought to haue bin made againſt the Conſul,	a. 1. 13.293.	*quòd in Conſulem facta putantur,*
at the requeſts of *Cato* and *Domitius :*	a. 1. 13.294.	Catone *& Domitio poſtulante :*
one,	a. 1. 13.295.	*vnum,*
that it is lawfull to ſearch the Magiſtrates :	a. 1. 13.296.	*vt apud Magiſtratus inquiri liceret :*
another,	a. 1. 13.297.	*alterum,*
what ſort of diuiders ſhould haue againſt the Commonwealth,	a. 1. 13.298.	*cuiuſmodi, diuiſores haberent aduerſo Rempublicam,*
But *Lurco* a Tribune of the people is abſolued,	a. 1. 13.299.	Lurco *autem Tribunus *Pl.*(a. 1. 13.299. a.) *ſolutus eſt,*
who began his Magiſtracie when the law of *Aelia* began,	a. 1. 13.299.a	*qui Magiſtratum ſimul cum lege* Aelia *inijt,*
both from the *Aelian,* and the *Fuſian* [Law]	a. 1. 13.300.	*&* Aelia *&* Fuſia.
that he might make the Law *de ambitu,*	a. 1. 13.301.	*vt legem de ambitu ferret,*
which hee a lame man hath publiſhed	a. 1. 13.302.	*quam ille*(a. 13.302. a.) *claudus homo promulgauit*

*pl.plebis.

with

with prosperitie.	a. 1.	13.302.a	*bono auspicio.*	
So	a. 1.	13.303.	*Ita*	
the time of Election is deferred till about the second of August.	a. 1.	13.304.	*comitia in ante* * I I. *Kalendas sext. dilata sunt.*	*I I. Secu dum. * Sext. sextiles.
This is new in the Law,	a. 1.	13.305.	*Noui est in lege hoc,*	
that,	a. 1.	13.306.	*vt,*	
he which hath promised money to the Tribe,	a. 1.	13.307.	*qui nummos in tribu pronuntiarit,*	
if he giue it not,	a. 1.	13.308.	*si non dederit,*	
is excused.	a. 1.	13.309.	*impunè sit.*	
[But] if hee shall giue it,	a. 1.	13.310.	*Sin dederit,*	
that hee be debtor to euery tribe 3000 *Sestertij* :	a. 1.	13.311.	*vt* (a.1.13. 311.a.) *singulis tribubus** HS. CIↃ CIↃ CIↃ.*debeat:*	* Sestertio. ter mille.
while he liueth,	a. 1.	13.311.a	*quoad viuat,*	
I said,	a. 1.	13.312.	*Dixi,*	
that *Publius Clodius* had heretofore obserued the Law :	a. 1.	13.313.	*hanc legem* *P.Clodium *iam antea seruasse:*	*P.Publius
and that he was also wont to promise,	a. 1.	13.314.	*pronuntiare etiam solitum esse,*	
and	a. 1.	13.315.	*&*	
not to giue.	a. 1.	13.316.	*non dare.*	

But

but	a. 1. 13.317.	*sed*	
heare you Sir :	a. 1. 13.318.	*heus tu :*	
see you not that Consulſhip of ours,	a. 1. 13.319.	*vidésne, conſulatum illum noſtrum,*	
which *Curio* in times paſt called a Deification,	a. 1. 13.320.	*quem* Curio *antea * ἀπο̇θέωσιν *vocabat,*	* Deificationem
if this man bee made [Conſull]	a. 1. 13.321.	*Si * hic factus erit ,*	* Sc. Lucius Afranius.
will become a mockerie?	a. 1. 13.322.	**fabam mimum futurum ?*	* fabę minimum.i.e. hylum
Wherefore,	a. 1. 13.323.	*Quare,*	
as I thinke,	a. 1. 13.324.	*vt opinor,*	
wee muſt play the Philoſophers,	a. 1. 13.325.	* φιλοσοφητίον,	* Philoſophandum
as thou doſt,	a. 1. 13.326.	*id quod tu facis,*	
and	a. 1. 13.327.	*&*	
ſhould wee not ſhunne theſe conſulſhips?	a. 1. 13.328.	*iſtos conſulatus non *ἱλαφητίον?*	* Faciendum more ceruorum.
Whereas you write vnto me,	a. 1. 13.329.	*Quod ad me ſcribis,*	
that you purpoſe not to goe into *Aſia :*	a. 1. 13.330.	*te in Aſiam ſtatuiſse non ire :*	
verily	a. 1. 13.331.	*equidem*	

I

I had rather you ſhould goe :	a. 1.	13.332.	*mallem vt ires :*
and	a. 1.	13.333.	*ac*
I feare,	a. 1.	13.334	*vereor,*
that ſome inconue-nience may riſe thereby :	a. 1.	13.335.	*ne quid in iſta re mi-nùs commodè fiat :*
But yet	a. 1.	13.336.	*Sed tamen*
I cannot blame your determinati-on,	a. 1.	13.337.	*non poſſum reprehen-dere conſilium tuum,*
eſpecially	a. 1.	13.338.	*praſertim*
ſeeing	a. 1.	13.339.	*cùm*
I my ſelfe am not gone into the Pro-uince.	a. 1.	13.340.	*egomet in Prouinci-am non ſim profectus.*
Wee ſhall content vs with your Epi-grams,	a. 1.	13.341.	*Epigrammatis tuis (a.1.13.341.a) con-tenti erimus.*
which you haue placed in *Amal-théo,*	a. 1.	13.341.a	*quæ in* Amalthéo *poſuiſti,*
the rather,	a. 1.	13.342.	*praſertim,*
in that *Chilius* alſo hath left vs , and *Archias* hath writ-ten nothing of vs :	a. 1.	13.343.	*cùm &* Chilius *nos reliquerit, &* Archi-as *nihil de me ſcrip-ſerit :*

and

and	a. 1.	13.344.	*ac*
I feare :	a. 1.	13.345.	*vereor,*
that *Lucullus* may now caſt an eye to the *Cæcilian* Fable ;	a. 1.	13.346.	*ne* Lucullus (a. 13. 346.a.b.)*nunc ad* Cæ-ciliana *fabula ſpectet* ;
becauſe	a. 1.	13.346.a	*quoniam*
he hath finiſhed the Greeke Poem,	a. 1.	13.346.b	*Græcum poëma condidit,*
I haue thanked *Antonius*	a. 1.	13.347.	Antonio (a. 1.13. 347.a.)*gratias egi,*
on your behalfe ;	a. 1.	13.347.a	*tuo nomine*
and	a. 1.	13.348.	(a.1.13.348.a.)*que*
I gaue the ſame Epiſtle to *Manlius.*	a. 1.	13.348.a	*eam* (a. 13. 148.) *epiſtola* Manlio *dedi.*
I wrote but ſeldom to you heretofore;	a. 1.	13.349.	*Ad te ideo antea rarius ſcripſi,*
becauſe I found no fit man to giue them vnto,	a. 1.	13.350.	*quòd non habebam idoneum, cui darem,*
neither did I well know,	a. 1.	13.351.	*nec ſatis ſciebam,*
what to giue.	a. 1.	13.352.	*quid darem.*
I thinke I am euen with you : [or] I haue payed you home.	a. 1.	13.353.	*te valdè vindicaui.*

If

If *Cincius* bring me any businesse of yours, I will vndertake it.	a. 1.	13.354.	Cincius, *si quid ad me tui negotij detulerit, suscipiam.*
But	a. 1.	13.355.	*Sed*
at this present	a. 1.	13.356.	*nunc*
hee is more imployed in his owne:	a. 1.	13.357.	*magis in suo est occupatus :*
wherein I am not wanting to him.	a. 1.	13.358.	*in quo ego ei non desum.*
Looke for often Letters from vs,	a. 1.	13.359.	*Tu* (a. 1.13.356.a.) *crebras à nobis litteras expecta,*
when you remaine certaine in any place :	a. 1.	13.359.a	*si vno in loco es futurus :*
but	a. 1.	13.360.	*ast*
see that you also send more.	a. 1.	13.361.	*pluries etiam ipse mittito.*
. I would haue you write vnto me	a. 1.	13.362.	*Velim ad me scribas*
in what fashion your *Amaltheum* is,	a. 1.	13.363.	*cuiusmodi sit* * ἀμαλθεῖον *tuum,*
how adorned,	a. 1.	13.364.	*quo ornatu,*
how the place is described :	a. 1.	13.365.	*qua* * τοποθησία.
and		13.366.	*&*
whatsoeuer Poems you haue,	a. 1.	13.367.	*quæ poëmata*(a.1.13. 367.b.c.)*habes,*

* Amaltheum.

* loci descriptione.

and

and	a. 1. 13.367.a	(a.1.13.367.b.) *què*
what Hiftories	a. 1. 13. 367 b	*quas* (a.1.13.367.a.) *hiftorias*
of *Amalthea,*	a. 1. 13.367.c	*de* * *ἀμαλθεία,*
fend them to me.	a. 1. 13.368.	*ad me mittas.*
I haue a minde to make one in *Ar-pinas.*	a. 1. 13.369.	*Lubet mihi facere in* Arpinati.
I will fend you fomething of that which I haue writ-ten:	a. 1. 13.370.	*Ego tibi aliquid de meis fcriptis mittam,*
there's nothing yet fully finifhed.	a. 1. 13.371.	*nihil erat abfoluti.*
Farewell.	a. 1. 13.372.	*Vale.*
A great variety of the will is fhew'd vnto me,	a. 1. 14. 1.	*Magna mihi varietas voluntatis* (a.1. 14. 1. a.b.c.)*demonftrata eft,*
and	a.1. 14.1. a	*&*
an alteration of the opinion and iudge-ment	a. 1. 14.1.b	*difsimilitudo opinio-nis & iudicij.*
of my brother *Quintus*	a. 1. 14.1. c	*Q. fratris mei*
out of your let-ters,	a. 1. 14. 2.	*ex litteris tuis,*
wherein	a.1. 14. 3.	*in quibus*
vnto me	a. 1. 14. 4.	*ad me*

* Amalthea.

Q. *Quint.*

you

you haue sent the copies of his letters.	a. 1. 14. 5.	*epiſtolarum illius exempla miſiſti.*
Whereupon	a. 1. 14. 6.	*Qua ex re*
I am both so much troubled with griefe,	a. 1. 14. 7.	*& moleſtia ſum tanta affeltus,*
as mine entire affection towards both of you ſhould bring me :	a. 1. 14. 8.	*quantam mihi meus amor ſummus erga vtrumque veſtrûm afferre debuit :*
and	a. 1. 14. 9.	*&*
with admiration,	a. 1. 14.10.	*admiratione,*
what ſhould haue happened,	a. 1. 14.11.	*quidnam accidiſſet,*
that ſhould bring my brother *Quintus* to bee ſo grieuouſly offended, or his mind ſo altered.	a. 1. 14.12.	*quod afferret * Q. fratri meo aut offenſionem tam grauem, aut commutationem tantam voluntatis.*
Indeede	a. 1. 14.13.	*Atque*
I had an incling of thus much heretofore,	a. 1. 14.14.	*illud à me iam ante intelligebatur,*
which I ſaw you alſo ſuſpected vpon your departure frõ vs,	a. 1. 14.15.	*quod te quoque ipſum diſcedentem à nobis ſuſpicari videbam,*

* *Q. Quintu*

that

that hee conceiued some bad opinion,	a. 1.	14.16.	*subeſſe neſcio quid opinionis incommoda,*
and	a. 1.	14.17.	*(a.1.14.17.a.) què*
that hee was diſcontented,	a. 1.	14.17.a	*ſaucium (a. 1. 14. 17.)eius animum,*
and	a. 1.	14.18.	*&*
that there were hatefull ſuſpitions betweene you.	a. 1.	14.19.	*inſediſſe quaſdam odioſas ſuſpiciones.*
which I deſiring to remedie	a. 1.	14.20.	*quibus ego mederi cùm cuperem*
both many times heretofore,	a. 1.	14.21.	*& antea ſæpè,*
and alſo more earneſtly	a. 1.	14.22.	*& vehementiùs etiam*
after the getting of the prouince :	a. 1.	14.23.	*poſt ſortitionem prouinciæ :*
I did neyther vnderſtand that hee was ſo much offended,	a. 1.	14.24.	*nec tantùm intelligebam ei eſſe offenſionis,*
as your letters declared :	a 1.	14.25.	*quantum litteræ tuæ declarant.*
neyther had I ſo good ſucceſſe,	a. 1.	14.26.	*nec tantum proficiebam,*
as I deſired :	a. 1.	14.27.	*quantum volebam :*
But yet	a. 1.	14.28.	*Sed tamen*
this was my comfort,	a. 1.	14.29.	*hoc me ipſe conſolabar,*

that

that	a. 1.	14.30.	*quòd*
I doubted not,	a. 1.	10.31.	*non dubitabam,*
but that he should see you :	a. 1.	14.32.	*quin te ille (a. 1. 14. 32. a. b. c.) visurus esset :*
eyther at *Dyrrachium*	a. 1.	14.32.a	*aut* Dyrrachij
or	a. 1.	14.32.b	*aut*
in some of those places;	a. 1.	14.52.c.	*in istis locis vspiam;*
which happening,	a. 1.	14.33.	*quod cùm accidisset,*
I was in hope	a. 1.	14.34.	*confidebam*
and	a. 1.	14.35.	*ac*
I perswaded my selfe,	a. 1.	14.36.	*mihi persuaseram,*
that it might fall out,	a. 1.	14.37.	*fore,*
that all matters would bee appeased betweene you,	a. 1.	14.38.	*vt omnia placarentur inter vos,*
not onely by discourse,	a. 1.	14.39.	*non modò sermone,*
and	a. 1.	14.40.	*ac*
by arguing,	a. 1.	14.41.	*disputatione,*
but	a. 1.	14.42.	*sed*
by seeing and accompanying each other:	a. 1.	14.43.	*aspectu ipso, congressúque vestro:*

For

For	a. 1. 14.44.	*Nam*
how much courte-fie is in my brother *Quintus*,	a. 1. 14.45.	*quanta fit in* *Q. fratre meo comitas*
how pleafing a na-ture	a. 1. 14.46.	*quanta iucunditas,*
how tender his minde is,	a. 1. 14.47.	*quàm mollis animus,*
as well to take of-fence, as to fhake it off,	a. 1. 14.48.	*& ad accipiendam, & ad deponendam of-fenfionem,*
it skills not	a. 1. 14.49.	*nihil attinet*
that I fhould write vnto you,	a. 1. 14.50.	*me ad te (a.1.14.50. a.) fcribere,*
who knoweft thofe things.	a. 1. 14.50.a	*qui ea nofti.*
But	a. 1. 14.51.	*Sed*
it falls out very crofly,	a. 1. 14.52.	*accidit perincommodè,*
that thou haft not feene him in any place.	a. 1. 14.53.	*quòd eum nufquam vidifti.*
for that hath been of more power,	a. 1. 14.54.	*valuit enim plus,*
that hath beene preffed vpon him	a. 1. 14.55.	*quod erat illi (a.1.14. 55.a.)inculcatum*
by the deuices of fome,	a. 1. 14.55.a	*artificijs nonnullo-rum,*

×Q. Quinto.

then

then	a. 1.	14.56.	quàm
eyther office,	a, 1.	14.57.	aut officium,
or	a. 1.	14.58.	aut
neereneſſe,	a. 1.	14.59.	neceſſitudo,
or that firſt loue of yours :	a. 1.	14.60.	aut amor veſter ille priſtinus :
which ſhould haue beene very power-full.	a. 1.	14.61.	qui plurimùm vale-re debuit.
And	a. 1.	14.62.	Atque
where the fault of this inconuenience reſteth,	a. 1.	14.63.	huius incommodi cul-pa vbi reſideat,
I can more eaſily i-magine,	a. 1.	14.64.	facilius poſſum exi-ſtimare,
then write.	a. 1.	14.65.	quàm ſcribere.
for I feare	a. 1.	14.66.	vereor enim,
that I ſhall not ſpare your [friends,]	a. 1.	14.67.	ne (a.1.14.67.a.)non parcam tuis,
while I defend mine.	a. 1.	14.67.a	dum defendam meos.
For	a. 1.	14.68.	Nam
I vnderſtand thus,	a. 1.	14.69.	ſic intelligo,
though your fami-lie were not the cauſe of any wound,	a. 1.	14.70.	vt nihil à domeſticis vulneris factum ſit,

yet

yet that,	a. 1.	14.71.	*illud quidem,*
that was,	a. 1.	14.72.	*quod erat,*
they might doubt-lesse haue heald.	a. 1.	14.73.	*eos certè sanare potuisse.*
But	a. 1.	14.74.	*Sed*
I will more com-modiously explaine the mischiefe of all this businesse vnto you at our mee-ting.	a. 1.	14.75.	*huiusce rei totius vi-tium* (a.1.14.75.a.b) *præsenti tibi commodi-ùs exponam.*
which is also a lar-ger distent,	a. 1.	14.75.a	*quod aliquantò etiam latiùs patet,*
then it appeareth,	a. 1.	14.75.b	*quàm videtur,*
of those letters	a. 1.	14.76.	*de his literis,*
which he sent vn-to you at *Thessalonica,*	a. 1.	14.77.	*quas ad te* Thessalo-nicam *misit,*
and		14.78.	*&*
of the speeches,	a. 1.	14.79.	*de sermonibus,*
which you thinke hee had	a. 1.	14.80.	*quos ab illo* (a.1.14. 80.a.b.c.d.e.) *habitos putas,*
both	a. 1.	14.80.a	*&*
at *Rome*	a. 1.	14.80.b	Romæ
with your friends,	a. 1.	14.80.c	*apud amicos tuos,*
and	a. 1.	14.80.e	*&*

in

in the iourney	a. 1.	34. 80. e	*in itinere*
I know no so great cause that he had.		14.81.	*ecquid tantùm causæ sit ignoro.*
But	a. 1.	14.82.	*Sed*
all the hope I haue lies in your humanity	a. 1.	14.83.	*omnis in tua posita est humanitate mihi spes*
of taking away this trouble.	a. 1.	14.84.	*huius leuandæ molestiæ.*
For	a. 1.	14.85.	*Nam,*
if you will [but] haue this opinion,	a. 1.	14.86.	*si ita statueris,*
that the mindes of the best men may both often bee stirred, and that the same may bee appeased,	a. 1.	14.87.	*& irritabiles animos esse optimorum sæpè hominum, & eosdem placabileis,*
and	a. 1.	14.88.	*&*
that this readines of nature proceeds most an end from a good disposition :	a. 1.	14.89.	*esse hanc agilitatem a.1.14.89.a.) mollitiémq; naturæ plerumque bonitati :*
(as I may so call it)	a. 1.	14.89.a	*vt ita dicam)*
and,	a. 1.	14.90.	*&,*
that which importeth	a. 1.	14.91.	*id quod caput est,*

that

that wee ought to tolerate any inconueniences, vices, or iniuries that shall fall out amongst vs :	a. 1.	14.92.	*nobis inter nos nostra, siue incommoda, siue vitia, siue iniurias esse tolerandas :*
those things will easily bee mitigated,	a. 1.	14.93.	*facilè hæc (a. 1.14. 93.a.)mitigabuntur,*
as I hope,	a. 1.	14.93.a	*quemadmodum spero.*
which I intreat you	a. 1.	14.94.	*quod ego, (a. 1. 14. 94.a.) te rogo*
that you will doe ;	a. 1.	14.94 a	*vt facias;*
for	a. 1.	14.95.	*nam*
it especially concernes me,	a. 1.	14.96.	*ad me (a.1.14.96.a.) maximè pertinet,*
who loue you singularly well,	a. 1.	14.96.a	*qui te vnicè diligo,*
that there is none of my friends,	a. 1.	14.97.	*neminem esse meorum,*
who either loues you nor,	a. 1.	14.98.	*qui aut te non amet,*
or	a. 1.	14.99.	*aut*
is not loued of you.	a. 1.	14.100.	*abs te non ametur.*
That part of your epistle was nothing necessarie,	a. 1.	14.101.	*Illa pars epistolæ tuæ minimè fuit necessaria,*

wherein

wherein you ex-preſſe,	a. 1. 14. 102.	*in qua exponis,*
what opportunities you haue omitted,	a. 1. 14. 103	*quas facultates* (a. 1. 14.103.a.b.c.d.e.a.) *prætermiſeris,*
either of Prouinciall, or of City promotions,	a. 1. 14.103.a	*aut Prouincialium, aut vrbanorum commodorum,*
as well	a. 1. 14.103.b	*&*
at other times,	a. 1. 13.103.c	*alijs temporibus,*
as	a. 1. 14.103. d	*et*
when I was Conſul:	a. 1. 14.203.e	*me ipſo Conſule:*
for	a. 1. 14.104.	(a. 1. 14.104.a) *enim*
both your integritie, and greatneſſe of minde is well knowne vnto me:	a. 1. 14.104.a	*mihi* (a. 1. 14. 104.) *perſpecta eſt & integritas, & magnitudo animi tui:*
neither did I hold that there was any difference at any time,	a. 1. 14.105.	*neque ego* (a. 1. 14. 105.a) *quicquam intereſſe vnquam duxi,*
betweene mee and thee,	a. 1. 14.105.a	*inter me atque te,*
beſides the courſe of life which it hath pleaſed vs to take:	a. 1. 14.106.	*præter voluntatem inſtituta vitæ:*
that	a. 1. 14.107.	*quòd*

a cer-

a certaine ambition led me to the defire of honour, and fome other reafon not to bee blamed, led thee to an honeft leifure :	a. 1. 14. 108.	*me ambitio quædam ad honorum ftudium, te autem alia minimè reprehendenda ratio ad honeftum otium duxit:*
but very commendable for vertue, induftry, and deuotion;	a. 1. 14. 109.	*vera quidem laude probitatis, diligentiæ, religionis;*
neither doe I put my felfe or any man before thee.	a. 1. 13. 110.	*neque me tibi, neque quenquam antepono.*
but for loue to me-ward,	a. 1. 14. 111.	*amoris verò erga me,*
excepting the loue of my brother, and thofe of my houfe,	a. 1. 14. 112.	*cùm à fraterno amore, domefticóque difceffi,*
I giue you the prize.	a. 1. 14. 113.	*tibi primas defero.*
for I haue feene,	a. 1. 14. 114.	*Vidi enim,*
I haue feene	a. 1. 14. 115.	*vidi,*
and	a. 1. 14. 116.	(a. 1. 14. 117. a.) *què*
I haue very well perceiued your forrowings & ioyings,	a. 1. 14. 116 a	*penitus* (a. 1. 14. 116.) *perfpexi* (a.1. 14. 116.b.) *& follicitudines, & lætitias tuas,*
in the diuerfities of my fortunes.	a. 1. 14. 116. b	*in meis varijs temporibus.*

Both

Both your congra-tulation, when wee were commended, was pleasing, and your côforting whê I was in feare, was welcome to me.	a. 1.	14.117.	*Fuit mihi fæpè & lau-dis noftra gratulatio tua iucunda , & timo-ris confolatio grata.*
Yea, at this pre-fent I am greatly de-ftitute,	a. 1.	14. 118.	*Quin mihi nunc* (a.1. 14.118. a.b.c.d. e.f.) *maximè deeft,*
you being abfent,		14.118. a	*te abfente,*
not onely [of] counfell	a. 1.	14.118. b	*non folùm confilium,*
wherein you are excellent ;	a.1.	14. 118. c	*quo tu excellis;*
but alfo	a. 1.	14.118.d	*fed etiam*
the intercourfe of talke,	a. 1.	14.118. e	*fermonis communica-tio,*
which was wont to be very delight-full to vs both.	a. 1.	14.118.f	*quæ mihi fuauiſſima tecum folet effe.*
What fhall I fay	a. 1.	14.119.	*Quid dicam*
in publike affaires?	a. 1.	14.120.	*in publica re?*
in which kinde	a. 1.	14.121.	*quo in genere*
I ought not to be negligent :	a. 1.	14.122.	*mihi negligenti effe non licet :*
or in pleading af-faires,	a. 1.	14.123.	*an in forenfi labore,*

which

which I heretofore suftained;	a. 1.	14.124.	quem antea (a.1.14. 125.a.) suftinebam;
for ambition,	a. 1.	14.124.a	propter ambitionem ,
now,	a. 1.	14.125.	nunc,
that by fauour I may maintain [my] dignity;	a. 1.	14. 1.6.	vt dignitatem tueri gratia poßim;
or in domesticke busineffes themselues?	a. 1.	14.127.	an in ipsis domesticis negotijs?
wherein	a.1.	14.128.	in quibus
I defire thee, and our difcourfes.	a. 1.	14.129.	ego(a.1.14.129. b. c.) te, sermonésque nostros desidero.
as well formerly,	a. 1.	14.129.a	cùm antea,
as alfo	a. 1.	14.129.b	tum verò
after the departure of my brother	a. 1.	14.129.c	post discessum fratris.
Laft of all [or in conclufion]	a. 1.	14.130.	Postremò
neither my paines, nor quiet, nor bufineffe, nor leifure nor affaires of the barre, nor of my houfe, nor publik, nor priuate } can longer want thy moft fweete and louing counfell and difcourfe.	a. 1.	14.131.	non labor meus, non requies, non negotium, non otium, non forenses res, non domesticæ, non publicæ, non priuatæ, } carere diutius tuo suauissimo, atque amantissimo con filio ac sermone possunt.

and

And	a. 1.	14.132.	*Atque*
the bashfulnesse of vs both hath often hindred the remembrance of these things.	a. 1.	14.133.	*harum rerum commemorationem verecundia sæpe impediuit vtriusque nostrûm.*
But at this present	a. 1.	14.134.	*nunc autem*
the same was necessarie	a. 1.	14.135.	*ea fuit necessaria*
for that part of thine epistle,	a. 1.	14.136.	*propter eam partem epistolæ tuæ,*
by which	a. 1.	14.137.	*per quam*
thou wast pleased to acquite and iustifie thy selfe and carriages to me.	a. 1.	14.138.	*te, ac mores tuos mihi purgatos, ac probatos esse voluisti.*
And	a. 1.	14.139.	*Atque*
in that discommoditie	a. 1.	14.140.	*in ista incommoditate*
of his alienated and offended minde,	a. 1.	14.141.	*alienati illius animi, & offensi,*
notwithstanding	a. 1.	14.142.	*(a. 1. 14. 142. a.) tamen*
there is this commoditie	a. 1.	14.142·a	*illud inest (a. 1. 14. 142.) commodi*
that	a. 1.	14.143.	*quòd*
both	a. 1.	14.144.	*&*

thy

thy pleafure about the leauing of the Prouince was known to me;	a. 1.	14. 145.	*mihi* (a.1.14.187.a. b.) *nota fuit* (a.1.14. 147.c.d.) *tua voluntas omittendæ Prouinciæ*;
and	a. 1.	14.145.a	*&*
to other your friends;	a. 1.	14.145.b	*cæteris amicis tuis,*
and	a. 1.	14.145. c	*&*
fometimes teftified by thy felfe,	a. 1.	14. 145.d	*abs te aliquando teftificata,*
that, it fhould feeme to proceed not from diffention, and ftrife betweene you, but from thine owne liking, and iudgement.	a. 1.	14. 146.	*vt,* (a.1.14. 148. a.) *non diffentione, ac diffidio veftro, fed voluntate, ac iudicio tuo factum effe videatur.*
that you are not together,	a. 1.	14.146.a	*quòd vnà non eftis,*
Wherefore	a. 1.	14. 147.	*Quare*
both	a. 1.	14.148.	*&*
thofe things fhall be pacified;	a. 1.	14. 149.	*illa* (a. 1. 14. 15 .a.) *expiabuntur;*
that haue been violated,	a. 1.	14.149.a	*quæ violata,*
and	a. 1.	14. 150.	*&*
thefe of ours fhall bee religioufly continued.	a. 1.	14. 151.	*hæc noftra,* (a. 1. 14. 151.a.) *fuam religionem obtinebunt.*

s c.funt.

which

which are moſt ho-lily conſerued[hi-therto,]	a. 1.	14.151.a	quæ ſunt ſanctiſsimè conſeruata,	
Wee are heere verſ'd,	a. 1.	14.152.	Nos hîc (a.1.14.152.a.) verſamur.	
in a crazie, miſera-ble, and changing Commonwealth	a. 1.	14,152.a	in * rep. infirma, mi-ſera, commutabilique	* republica.
For I beleeue,	a. 1.	14.153.	Credo enim	
that you haue heard,	a. 1.	14.154.	te audiſſe,	
that our Knights are almoſt diuided from the ſenate:	a. 1.	14.155.	noſtros Equites pænè à ſenatu eſſe diſiunctos :	
who firſt tooke this very hainouſly,	a. 1.	14.156.	qui primùm illud valdè grauiter tule-runt,	
that it was publi-ſhed	a. 1.	14.157.	promulgatum (a.1.14.157.a.) fuiſſe	
by the Senats order,	a. 1.	14.157.a	ex * S. * C.	* S Senatus * Conſulto.
that there ſhould be an examination.	a. 1.	14.158.	vt (a.1.14.160.a.b.) quæreretur.	
about them,	a. 1.	14.158.a	de ijs,	
which had receiued a bribe of[money,]	a. 1.	14.158.b	qui (a.1.14.158.c.) pecuniam accepiſſent,	
for their iudgement [or ſentence.]	a. 1.	14.158.c	ob iudicandum	
In the diſcuſſing of which buſineſſe,	a. 1.	14.159.	Qua in re decernen-da,	

I

I by chance not being prefent,	a. 1. 14.160.	cùm ego cafu non affuiſſem,
and	a. 1. 14.161.	(a.1.14.161.) què
hauing heard	a. 1. 14. 161. a	ſenſiſſem
that the order of the knights was diſpleaſed thereat,	a. 1. 14.162.	id equeſtrem ordinem ferre moleſtè,
and yet did not publikely ſpeake ſo much,	a. 1. 14.163.	neque apertè dicere,
I reprehended the Senate,	a. 1. 14. 164.	obiurgaui Senatum,
as I thought,	a.1. 14.165.	vt mihi viſus ſum,
with great authority,	a. 1. 14.166.	ſumma cum auctoritate,
and	a. 1. 14.167.	&
in a cauſe that was ſhameleſſe,	a. 1. 14.168.	in cauſa non verecunda,
I was very graue and copious.	a. 1. 14.169.	admodùm grauis, & copioſus fui.
Behold, other importunate deſires of the knights, ſcarce to be tolerated,	a. 1. 14.170.	Ecce, aliæ deliciæ equitum vix ferendæ,
which I did not onely tolerate,	a. 1. 14.171.	quas ego non ſolùm tuli,
but I fauoured alſo.	a. 1. 14.172.	ſed etiam ornaui.

The

The (cuſtomers) of Aſia complained	a. 1.	14.173.	*Aſiani,* (a.1.14.173. a.) *queſti ſunt*
who were farmers to the cenſors,	a. 1.	14.173.a	*qui ae cenſoribus conduxerunt,*
in the Senate,	a. 1.	14.174	*in Senatu,*
that they had farmed [their places] at too great a rate:	a. 1.	14.175.	*ſe* (a. 1.14.175.a.) *nimiùm magno conduxiſſe:*
being deceiued by couetouſneſſe,	a. 1.	14.175.a	*cupiditate prolapſos,*
their requeſt was that the beaſe might be made voide.	a. 1.	14.176.	*vt induceretur locatio, poſtulauerunt.*
I was chiefe of thoſe that fauoured them,	a. 1.	14.177.	*Ego princeps in adiutoribus,*
or rather the ſecond.	a. 1.	14.178.	*atque adeò ſecundus.*
For,	a. 1.	14.179.	*Nam,*
that they durſt make this demand,	a. 1.	14.180.	*vt illi auderent hoc poſtulare,*
Craſſus put them forward.	a. 1.	14.181.	*Craſſus eos impulit,*
The thing was odious,	a. 1.	14.182.	*Inuidioſa res,*
a ſhameleſſe requeſt,	a. 1.	14.183.	*turpis poſtulatio,*
and	a. 1.	14.184.	*&*

a

a confeſſion of an open raſhneſſe.	a. 1. 14.185.	confeſſio temerita-tis.
there was great danger,	a. 1. 14.186.	ſummum erat periculum,
leſt they might be altogether alienated from the Senate,	a. 1. 14.187.	ne, (a.1.14.187.a.) planè alienarentur à Senatu,
if they had obtained nothing.	a. 1. 14.187.a	ſi nihil impetraſſent.
Hereunto alſo we gaue greatly our helping hands,	a. 1. 14.188.	Huic quoque rei ſubuentum eſt maximè à nobis,
and,	a. 1. 14.189.	(a. 1. 14. 189.a.) què,
brought things to that paſſe,	a. 1. 14.189. a	perfectum,
that they had a very full Senate , and very willing to giue them audience,	a. 1. 14.191.	vt frequentiſſimo Senatu, & libentiſſimo vterentur,
and	a. 1. 14.192.	què
I ſpake many things	a. 1. 14.192.a	multa(a.1.14.192.a) à me (a.1.14.192.b.) dicta ſunt
of the dignity and concord of the orders [of the Senate and Caualiers]	a. 1. 14.192. b	de ordinum dignitate, & concordia

on the Kalends of December.	a. 1.	14.*193.*	*Kalendis* * *Decembr.*
and	a. 1.	14.194.	*&*
the day following;	a. 1.	14.195.	*postridie;*
neither is the busi-neſſe as yet ended:	a. 1.	14.196.	*neque adhuc res confecta eſt:*
but	a. 1.	14.197.	*ſed*
the Senates plea-ſure is perceiued.	a. 1.	14.198.	*voluntas Senatus perſpecta.*
For	a. 1.	14.199.	*(a.1.14.199.a.) Enim*
Metellus the ele-cted Conſul onely had oppoſed;	a. 1.	14.199. a	*vnus(a.1.14.199.a.) contrà dixerat Metellus* * *Coſ.* *deſign.*
Our great *Cato* was to haue made a long ſpeech,	a. 1.	14.200.	*Diu erat dicturus (a. 1.14.200.a.) heros ille noſter,* Cato,
(to whoſe turne it came not)	a.1.	14.200.a	*(ad quem (a.1.14. 200.b.) peruentum non eſt*
by reaſon of the ſhortnes of the day.	a. 1.	14.200.b	*propter diei breuitatem.*
In this ſort	a. 1.	14.201.	*Sic*
continuing my pur-poſe, and appoint-ment,	a. 1.	14.202.	*ego conſeruans rationem inſtitutionémque noſtram,*
I maintaine that concord which I compoſed,	a. 1.	14.203.	*tueor (a.1.14.203. a.) illam à me conglutinatam concordiam,*

as

as I am able.	a. 1.	14.203.a	*vt poſſum.*
But yet,	a. 1.	14.204	*Sed tamen,*
becauſe theſe things are weake,	a. 1.	14.205.	*quoniam iſta ſunt infirma,*
we haue a certaine ſafe way made good vnto vs,	a. 1.	14.206.	*munitur quædã nobis* (a.1.14.206.a.) *tuta* (a.1.14.206.b.) *via,*
to keepe our fortunes,	a. 1.	14.260.a	*ad retinendas opes noſtras,*
as I ſuppoſe,	a.1.	14.206.b	*vt ſpero,*
which I cannot ſufficiently explaine vnto you by letters:	a. 1.	14.207.	*quam tibi litteris ſatis explicare non poſſum:*
yet	a. 1.	14.208.	(a.1.14.208.a.)*tamẽ*
I will giue you a glimmering of it.	a. 1.	14.208.a	*ſignificatione parua oſtendã* (a.1.14.208.)
I am very great with *Pompeius.*	a. 1.	14.209.	*Vtor* Pompeio *familiariſſimè.*
I know what you'l ſay.	a. 1.	14.210.	*Video, quid dicas.*
I will looke to the maine chance:	a. 1.	14.211.	*Cauebo, quæ ſunt cauenda:*
I'le write more another time	a. 1.	14.212.	*ſcribã aliâs* (a.1.14.212.a.b.)*plura.*
vnto you,	a. 1.	14.212.a	*ad te,*

of what I thinke concerning the vn- dertaking the go- uernement of the Common-wealth:	a. 1.	14.212. b	_de meis confilijs ca- peffenda* reip._
know	a. 1.	14.213.	(a.1.14.213.a.) _fcito_
that _Lucceius_ inten- deth	a. 1.	14.213.a	Lucceium (a.1.14. 213.a.b.)_habere in a- nimo_
out of hand to de- mand the Conful- fhip.	a. 1.	14.213.b	_confulatum_ (a.1.14. 214.a.) _ftatim petere._
for	a. 1.	14.214.	(a.1. 14.214.a.) _e- nim_
they fay there are onely two that were to ftand for it.	a. 1.	14.114.a	_duo_ (a.1.14.214.) _foli dicuntur petituri._
Cefar thinkes to ioyne with him:	a. 1.	14.215.	Cæfar _cum eo coire_ (a.1.14.215.a.)_cogi- tat:_
through _Arrius:_	a. 1.	14.215.a	_per_ Arrium:
and	a. 1.	14.216.	_&_
Bibulus makes ac- count that he may be ioyned	a. 1.	14.217.	Bibulus (a.1.14. 217.a.) _fe putat_ (.a.1. 14.217.b.) _poffe con- iungi_
with this man	a. 1.	14.217.a	_cum hoc_
by meanes of _Ca- ius Pifo:_	a. 1.	14.217.b	_per_ Caium Pifo- nem:

Laugheft

*Reipubli

Laugheſt thou?	a. 1.	14.218.	*Rides?*
Theſe are not things to laugh at,		14.119.	*Non ſunt hæc ridicula,*
beleeue me.	a. 1.	14.120.	*mihi crede.*
What elſe ſhall I write vnto thee?	a. 1.	14.121.	*Quid aliud ſcribam ad te?*
What?	a. 1.	14.222.	*Quid?*
there are many things.	a. 1.	14.223.	*multa ſunt:*
But	a. 1.	14.224.	*Sed*
[wee will keepe them] till another time.	a. 1.	14.225.	*in aliud tempus.*
If thou wouldeſt haue vs expect thee,		14.226.	*Te, ſi expectari velis,*
take order	a. 1.	14.227.	*cures,*
that I may know [as much.]	a. 1.	14.228.	*vt ſciam.*
At this preſent	a. 1.	14.229.	*Iam*
I modeſtly requeſt that	a. 1.	14.230.	*illud modeſtè rogo,*
which I ſpecially deſire,	a. 1.	14.231.	*quod maximè cupio,*
that you would come ſpeedily,	a. 1.	14.232.	*vs quamprimùm venias,*

on the Nones of December:	a. 1.	14.233.	*Nonis* * *Decembr.*
Farewell.	a. 1.	14.234.	*Vale.*
I want nothing more at this pre-sent,	a. 1.	15.1.	*Nihil mihi nunc scito tam deesse,*
than	a. 1.	15.2.	*quàm*
that man,	a. 1.	15.3.	*hominem eum,*
with whom I might communicate	a. 1.	15.4.	*quicũ omnia (a. 1.15. 4.a.) vnà cõmunicem*
the things that trouble me,	a. 1.	15.4.a.	*quæ me curâ aliquâ afficiunt,*
that would loue me,	a. 1.	15.5.	*qui me amet,*
that would bee wise,	a. 1.	15.6.	*qui sapiat,*
with whom I might conuerse:	a. 1.	15.7.	*quicum ego collo-quar :*
I neede faine no-thing,	a. 1.	15.8.	*nihil fingam,*
I neede not dif-semble,	a. 1.	15.9.	*nihil difsimulem,*
I neede hide no-thing.	a. 1.	15.10.	*nihil obtegam.*
for	a. 1.	15.11.	*(a.1.15.12.a.) enim*

* Decemb

my

my moſt ſimple-hearted and louing brother *Metellus* is abſent,	a. 1. 15.11.a.	*abeſt*(a.1.15.11.)*fraͤ ter ὁμιλίσατ⊙ & amantiſsimus* Metellus,
which is not a man,	a. 1. 15.12.	*non homo,*
but	a. 1. 15.13.	*ſed*
the Sea-ſide,	a. 1. 15.14.	*littus,*
and	a. 1. 15.15.	*atque*
ayre	a. 1. 15.16.	*aër,*
and	a. 1. 15.17.	*&*
meere ſolitarineſſe.	a. 1. 15.18.	*ſolitudo mera.*
But thou, where art thou?	a. 1. 15.19.	*Tu autem* (a. 1. 15. 19. a. b. c.) *vbinam es?*
who didſt often take away my care and vexation of minde,	a. 1. 15.19.a.	*qui ſæpiſsimè curam, & angorem animi mei,* (a. 15. 19. b) *leuâ-ſti,*
by thy ſpeech and counſell,	a. 1. 15.19.b	*ſermone & conſilio* (a. 1.15.19.a.)*tuo,*
who waſt to bee vnto me,	a. 1. 15.19.c	*qui mihi* (a. 1. 15. 19.d. e.f. g. h.i.) *eſſe ſoles,*
as well	a. 1. 15.19.d	*&*

a com-

a companion in Publike affaires,	a. 1.	15.19.e	*in publica re focius,*
as	a. 1.	15.19.f	*&*
priuy to all my priuate bufineffe;	a.1.	15.19.g	*in priuatis omnibus confcius;*
and	a. 1.	15.19.h	*&*
partaker of all my difcourfes and determinations.	a. 1.	15.19.i	*omnium meorum fermonum & confiliorum particeps.*
I am fo deftitute,	a. 1.	15.20.	*Ita fum deftitutus,*
that I haue fo much quiet time,	a. 1.	15.21.	*vt tantùm requietis habeam,*
as is fpent	a. 1.	15.22.	*quantum*(a.1.15.22. a.b.c.d.e.)*confumitur*
with my wife,	a. 1.	15.22.a	*cum vxore,*
and	a. 1.	15.22.b	*&*
my daughter,	a. 1.	15.22. c	*filiola,*
and	a. 1.	15.22.d	*&*
my fweet *Cicero.*	a. 1.	15.22. e	*mellito* Cicerone.
For	a. 1.	15.23.	*Nam*
thofe our ambitious and painted friendfhips, giue vs a kinde of reputatió abroad,	a. 1.	15.24.	*illa ambitiofæ noftræ, fucofæq; amicitiæ, funt in quodam fplendore forenfi,*
they are fruitleffe at home.	a. 1.	15.25.	*fructum domefticum non habent.*
Therefore	a. 1.	15.26.	*Itaque*
when the houfe is well filled,	a. 1.	15.27.	*cùm bene completa domus eft,*

in the morning :	a. 1. 15.28.	*tempore matutino :*
when we go down to the forum,	a. 1. 15.29.	*cùm ad forum* (a. 1. 15.29.a.) *defcendimus,*
accompanied with troopes of friends,	a. 1. 15.29. a	*ftipati gregibus amicorum,*
we can finde none,	a. 1. 15.30.	*reperire* (a. 1.15.30. a.) *neminem poffumus,*
of that great troope,	a. 1. 15.30. a	*ex magna turba,*
with whom wee may either freely fport our felues, or breathe familiarly.	a. 1. 15.31.	*quicum aut iocari liberè, aut fufpirare familiariter pofsimus.*
Wherefore	a. 1. 15.32.	*Quare*
we expect thee,	a. 1. 15.33.	*te expectamus,*
we long for thee,	a. 1. 15.34.	*te defideramus,*
yea at this prefent we call thee.	a. 1. 15.35.	*te iam etiam arcefsimus.*
For,	a. 1. 15.36.	(a.1.15.36.a.) *enim,*
there are many things	a. 1. 15.36. a	*Multa funt* (a. 1.15. 36.)
which vexe and trouble me:	a. 1. 15.37.	*quæ me follicitant angúntque:*
which methinkes I fhould bee able to draw forth.	a. 1. 15.38.	*quæ mihi videor* (a.1. 15.38.a.b.) *exhaurire poffe.*
if I had thine eare,	a. 1. 15.38.a	*aureis nactus tuas,*

in

in the difcourfe of one walke.	a. 1.	15.38.b	*vnius ambulationis fermone.*
And	a. 1.	15.39.	*Ac*
I will hide all the ftings and fcruples of domeftick cares:	a. 1.	15.40.	*domefticarum quidem follicitudinum aculeos omneis & fcrupulos occultabo :*
neither will I commit [them]	a. 1.	15.41.	*neque ego (a.1.15.41. a.b.c.) committam*
to this Epiftle,	a. 1.	15.41.a	*huic epiftolæ,*
and	a. 1.	15.41.b	*atque*
to an vnknowne meffenger.	a. 1.	15.41.c	*ignoto tabellario.*
And	a. 1.	15.42.	*Atque*
thefe are not very troublefome :	a. 1.	15.43.	*hi (a.1.15.42.b.)non funt permolefti :*
for	a.1.	15.43.a	*(a.1.15.42.b.)enim*
I will not haue thee to be moued.	a. 1.	15.43.b	*nolo (a. 1.15.42.a.) te permoueri.*
But	a. 1.	15.44.	*Sed*
notwithftanding	a. 1.	15.45.	*tamen*
they fit neere me,	a. 1.	15.46.	*infident,*
and	a. 1.	15.47.	*&*
trouble me,	a. 1.	15.48.	*vrgent,*
and	a. 1.	15.49.	*&*
they are not quiet vpon the coufell or difcourfe of any friend.	a. 1.	15.50.	*nullius amantis confilio aut fermone requiefcunt.*

But

But in publike bu-finesse,	a. 1.	15.51.	*In rep.* * *verò,*	* Republica.
though my minde be vpon them,	a. 1.	15.52.	*quanquam animus est præsens,*	
yet	a. 1.	15.53.	*tamen*	
my very will exceedingly fayleth me.	a. 1.	15.54.	*voluntas etiam, atq; etiam ipsa me deficit.*	
For	a. 1.	15.55.	*Nam*	
as I shall briefely collect those things,	a. 1.	15.56.	*vt ea breuiter (a.1.15.56.a.) colligam,*	
which haue beene done since your departure,	a. 1.	15:56.a	*quæ post tuum discessum acta sunt,*	
you will presently of necessitie cry out,	a. 1.	15.57.	*iam exclames necesse est,*	
that the Romane state can no longer continue.	a. 1.	15.58.	*res Romanas diutiùs stare non posse.*	
For	a. 1.	15.59.	*Etenim*	
after your going hence,	a. 1.	15.60.	*post profectionem tuam,*	
the *Clodian* Comedy cóming on the stage was first in cause	a. 1.	15.61.	*primus (a.1.15.61.a.) introitus fuit in causam fabulæ Clodianæ*	
(as I thinke)	a. 1.	15.61.a	*(vt opinor)*	
wherein	a. 1.	15.62.	*in qua*	
I was vehement,	a. 1.	15.63.	*Ego (a.1.15.63.a.b. c.d.e.) vehemens fui,*	

hauing

hauing opportuni-tie offered me	a. 1.	15.63.a	*nactus* (a.1. 15.63. b.) *locum*
(as I thought)	a. 1.	15.63.b	(*vt mihi videbar*)
of cutting off of luft,	a. 1.	15.63.c	*refecandæ libidinis,*
and	a. 1.	15.63.d	*&*
of bridling youth,	a. 1.	15.63.e	*coërcendæ iuuentutis,*
and	a. 1.	15.64.	*&*
I vfed all the powers	a. 1.	15.65.	*omneis profudi vireis*
of my mind & wit,	a. 1.	15.66.	*animi atq; ingenij mei,*
not drawne by ha-tred of any,	a. 1.	15.67.	*non odio adductus a-licuius,*
but	a. 1.	15.68.	*fed*
by hope,	a. 1.	15.69.	*fpe,*
not of correcting, but of healing the Citie.	a. 1.	15.70.	*non corrigendæ, fed fanandæ ciuitatis.*
The Common-wealth is afflicted	a.1.	15.71.	*Afflicta* * *refp.eft*
by bought and defiled iuftice.	a. 1.	15.72.	*empto conftupratóque iudicio.*
Marke,	a. 1.	15.73.	*Vide,*
what followed af-ter.	a. 1.	15.74.	*quæ fint poftea confe-cuta.*
He was made our Conful,	a. 1.	15.75.	*Conful eft impofitus is nobis,*

*refpublica.

whom

whom no man could behold,	a. 1. 15.76.	*quem nemo* (a.1. 15. 76.a.) *adspicere* (a. 1. 15.76.b.) *posset.*
but wee that were Philofophers,	a. 1. 15.76.a	*præter nos Philofophos,*
without fighing.	a. 1. 15.76.b	*fine fufpirio.*
What a wound was this?	a. 1. 15.77.	*Quantum hoc vulnus ?*
when the decree of the fenate was made;	a. 1. 15.78.	*facto* * S. *C.	*S Senatus. * Confulto.
about *ambitus,*	a. 1. 15.79.	*de ambitu,*
about matter of iuftice,	a. 1. 15.80.	*de iudicijs,*
nothing was inacted :	a. 1. 15.80.a	*nulla lex perlata :*
the fenate was difturbed,	a. 1. 15.81.	*exagitatus fenatus,*
the Romane nobilitie alienated :	a. 1. 15.82.	*alienati equites* R.*	*Romani.
fo that	a. 1. 15.83.	*fic*
that yeere ouerthrew two principall points that vpheld the Commonwealth,	a. 1. 15.84.	*ille annus duo firmamenta* reip.* (a.1. 15. 84.a.) *euertit;*	* reipublicę.
by mee alone conftituted.	a. 1. 15.84.a	*per me vnum conftituta.*
For	a. 1. 15.85.	*Nam*

both

both	a. 1.	15.86.	&
he neglected the authoritie of the senate,	a. 1.	15.87.	*senatus auctoritatem abiecit,*
and	a. 1.	15.88.	&
he disioyned the concord of the orders:	a. 1.	15.89.	*ordinum concordiam disiunxit:*
now	a. 1.	15.90.	(a.1.15.89.a.) *nunc*
Commeth heere that excellent yeere.	a. 1.	15.90.a	*Instat hîc* (a. 1. 15. 89.a) *ille annus egregius.*
the beginning thereof was of this sort,	a. 1.	15.91.	*eius initium eiusmodi fuit,*
that the annuall feasts of the youth should not be celebrated.	a. 1.	15.92.	*vt anniuersaria sacra iuuentutis non committerentur.*
For	a. 1.	15.93.	*Nam*
Memmius entred the wife of *Marcus Lucullus.*	a. 1.	15.94.	Marci Luculli *vxorem* Memmius (a. 1. 15. 94.a) *initiauit.*
at the celebration of his sacrifices	a. 1.	15.94.'a	*suis sacris*
Menelaus made a diuorce,	a. 1.	15.95.	Menelaus (a. 1.15. 95.a.) *diuortium fecit,*

taking

taking it very ill,	a. 1. 15.95.a.	*ægrè id paſſus,*	
although the Idæan paſtor contemned *Menelaus* onely:	a. 1. 15.96.	*quamquam ille* paſtor Idæus Menelaum ſolùm contempſerit:*	*Paris
this our *Paris* hath aſwell ſlighted *Menelaus* as *Agamemnon.*	a. 1. 15.97.	*hic noſter Paris tam* Menelaum, *quàm* Agamemnonem, *liberum non putauit.*	
but	a. 1. 15.98.	(a.1. 15.98.a.) *autem*	
there is one *Caius Herennius,*	a. 1. 15.98.a.	*eſt* (a. 1. 15.98.) *** C. Herennius *quidam,*	* Caius.
a Tribune of the people,	a. 1. 15.99.	*tribunus * pleb.*	*Plebis.
whom thou neuer kneweſt perhaps,	a. 1. 15.100.	*quem tu fortaſſe ne noſti quidem,*	
although	a. 1. 15.101.	*tametſi*	
you may haue knowne him.	a. 1. 15.102.	*potes noſſe.*	
for	15.103.	(a.1. 15. 103.a.) *enim*	
He is of your tribe:	a. 1. 15.103.a	*Tribulis* (a.1.15. 103.) *tuus eſt:*	

his

his father *Sextus* was wont to diuide money vnto you.	a. 1. 15. 104.	Sextus, *pater eius, nummos vobis diuidere solebat.*
He puts *Publius Clodius*	a. 1. 15. 105.	Is (a. 1.15.105.a.) Publium Clodium *traducit*
in the number of the Plebeans:	a· 1. 14.105.a	*ad plebem:*
and	a. 1. 15.106.	(a.1.15.106.a.)*qué*
the fame man propoundeth	a. 1. 14.106.a	*Idem* (a.1.15.106.) *fert*
that all the people giue their voices	a. 1.15. 107.	*vt vniuerfus populus* (a.1.15.107.a.) *fuf. fragium* (a.1.15.107. b.) *ferat.*
in Campus *Martius*	a. 1. 15.107. a	*in Campo* Martio
vpon the bufineffe of *Clodius.*	a. 1. 14.107. b	*de re* Clodij.
This man I entertained	a. 1. 15.108.	*Hunc ego accepi*
in the Senate,	a. 1. 15. 109.	*in Senatu,*
as I was wont:	a. 1. 15.110.	*vt foleo :*
but	a. 1. 15.111.	*fed*
he is the floweft man that liues.	a. 1. 15.112.	*nihil eft illo homine lentius.*
Metellus is an excellent conful,	a. 1. 15.113.	Metellus *eft conful egregius,*
and	a. 1. 15.114.	*&*
he loues vs :	a. 1. 15.115.	*nos amat:*

but

but	a. 1.	15.116.	*fed*
he hath wronged his reputation,	a. 1.	15.117.	*imminuit auctoritatem suam,*
that he hath a published caufe,	a. 1.	15.118.	*quòd habet* (a.1.15. 118. a.) *caufam promulgatam,*
as he reporteth	a. 1.	15.118.a	*vt dicit*
the fame of *Clodius.*	a. 1.	15.119.	*Illud idem de* Clodio.
but	a. 1.	15.120.	(a.1.15.220.a.) *autem*
the fonne of *Aulus,*	a. 1.	15.120.a	Auli (a. 1.15. 220.) *filius,*
O immortall gods,	a. 1.	15.121.	*ò dij immortales,*
how flow a Souldier	a. 1.	15.122.	*quàm ignauus* (a.1. 15.122.a.b.) *miles*
and	a. 1.	15.122.a	*&*
cowardly,	a. 1.	15.122.b	*fine animo,*
how worthy (is he)	a. 1.	15.123.	*quàm dignus,*
that *Palicanus* fhuld reuile him?	a. 1.	15.124.	*qui* Palicano (a.1. 15.124.a.)*os ad malè audiendum* (a.1.15. 124.a.) *prabeat?*
as he doth	a.1.	15.124.a	*ficut facit,*
daily.	a. 1.	15.204.b	*quotidiè.*
but	a. 1.	15.125.	(a.1.15.125.a.) *autem*

th-

the law Agraria in sooth but flight is propofed	a. 1. 15. 125.a	*Agraria* (a.1.15. 125.) *promulgata eft* (a.1.15. 125.b,) *fanè lenis:*
by *Flauius*,	a. 1. 15.125.b	*à* Flauio,
almoft the fame that the law Plotia.	a. 1. 15.126.	*eadem ferè quæ fuit Plotia.*
but	a. 1. 15.127.	*fed*
in the meane while	a. 1. 15.128.	*interea*
to be plaine, ther's not a politician to be found or dreamt of.	a. 1. 15.129.	* πολιτικὸς ἀνὴρ οὐδ'ὁταν *quifquam inueniri poteft.*
Our familiar friend *Pompeius*, who was able, is content to enioy his painted gowne and fay nothing.	a. 1. 15.130.	*qui poterat, familiaris nofter* (a.1.15.130. a.b.) Pompeius *togulam illam pictam filentio tuetur fuam.*
for he is fo our familiar friend :	a. 1. 15.130.a	*fic eft enim :*
[and] I would haue thee know as much	a. 1. 14.130. b	*volo te hoc fcire*
Craffus fpeakes not a word to difpleafe any man.	a. 1. 15. 131.	Craffus *verbum nullum contra gratiam.*

The

* Politicu vir ne ir fomnio qu dem.

the reſt you alrea-dy know:	a. 1.	15.132.	cæteros iam noſti:
who are ſuch fooles,	a. 1.	15.133.	qui ita ſunt ſtulti,
that they ſeeme to hope,	a. 1.	15.134.	ut (a.1.15.134.a.) ſperare uideantur,
though the Common-wealth were loſt,	a. 1.	15.134.a	amiſſa * rep.
that their fiſh-ponds ſhall be ſafe.	a. 1.	15.134.b	piſcinas ſuas fore ſaluas,
There is onely Ca-to	a. 1.	15.135.	Vnus eſt (a.1.15.135.a.b.c.d.e.) Cato
who lookes vnto it,	a. 1.	15.135.a	qui curet,
rather with con-ſtancie and integre-tie.	a. 1.	15.135.b	conſtantiâ magis, & integritate,
then	a. 1.	15.135.c	quàm
[for ought that I ſee]	a. 1.	15.135.d	(ut mihi videtur)
with counſell, or wit,	a. 1.	15.135.e	conſilio, aut ingenio,
who hath now theſe three moneths perſecuted the poore ſearchers or tole-maſters,	a. 1.	14.136.	qui miſeros publica-nos (a. 1.15. 136.a.) tertium iam menſem vexat,

* Republica.

who

who were his very friends,	a. 1. 15.136.a	*quos habuit amantißimos sui,*
neither doth hee suffer [them]	15.137.	*neque (a.1.15.137. a.) patitur*
to haue any answer	a. 1. 15.137.a	*ijs (.a.1.15.137. b.) responsum dari*
from the Senate	a. 1. 15. 137.b	*à Senatu*
so that	a. 1. 15.138.	*ita*
we are inforced to determine nothing.	a. 1. 15.139.	*nos cogimur (a.1.15. 139.a.) nihil decernere.*
of other busineſſe,	a. 1. 15.139.a	*reliquis de rebus,*
till the Searchers are answered.	a. 1. 15.140.	*antequàm publicanis responsum sit.*
wherefore	a. 1. 15.141.	*quare*
I make account,	a. 1. 15.142.	*(a.1.15.142.a.)puto*
that the Embaſies will be deferred alſo.	a. 1. 15.142.a	*etiam legationes reiectum iri (a. 1. 15. 142.)*
Now	a. 1. 14.145.	*Nunc*
thou see'st,	a. 1. 15.146.	*vides,*
with what waues we are toſſed.	a. 1. 15.147.	*quibus fluctibus iactemur*
though	a. 1. 15.148.	*etſi*
by thoſe things,	a. 1. 15.149.	*ex ijs,*
which wee haue written,	a. 1. 15.150.	*quæ scripſimus,*

yet,

yet, on tother fide	a. 1.	15.151.	*tamen etiam,*
thou doft not fee that I haue written them.	a. 1.	15.152.	*à me non ſcripta perſpicis.*
Come at length to fee how we doe :	a. 1.	15.153.	*Reuiſe nos aliquando:*
and	a. 1.	15.154.	*&*
although theſe affaires are to be ſhunned,	a. 1.	15.155.	*quanquam ſunt hæc fugienda,*
whither I call thee:	a. 1.	15.156.	*quò te voco:*
yet	a. 1.	15.157.	*tamen*
fee	a. 1.	15.158.	*fac*
that you efteeme ſo much of our loue,	a. 1.	15.159.	*vt amorem noſtrum tanti æſtimes,*
that you come thither,	a. 1.	15.160.	*vt eò,* (a.1.15.160 a) *peruenire velis,*
though it be with the troubles.	a. 1.	14.160. a	*vel cum his moleſtijs.*
For,	a.1.	15.161.	*Nam,*
that you bee not taxed in your abſence,	a. 1.	15.162.	*ne abſens cenſeare,*
I will procure that there be an edict made and put vp	a. 1.	15.163.	*curabo edicendum & proponendum*
in all places,	a. 1.	15.164.	*locis omnibus,*
but	a. 1.	15.165.	(a.1.15.165.a.) *autem*

to be taxed euery fiue yeeres,	a. 1.	15.165.a	*sub lustrum* (a. 1.15. 165.) *censeri,*
fauours altogether of the Merchant.	a. 1.	15.166.	*germani negotiatoris est.*
Wherefore	a. 1.	14.167.	*Quare*
bring things so about,	a. 1.	15.168.	*cura,*
that we may forth-with see you.	a. 1.	14.169.	*vt te quamprimùm videamus.*
Farewell.	a. 1.	15.170.	*Vale.*
on the eleuenth of the Kalends of Februarie.	a. 1.	15.171.	XI. *Kalendis* * *Febr.*
Quintus Metellus, and *Lucius Afranius* being Conſuls.	a. 1.	14.172.	* Q. Metello, * L. Afranio * Coſſ.
I ſhould exceede you,	a. 1.	16.1.	(a.16.1.a.b.c.d.e.f.) *te superarem,*
not onely,	a. 1.	16.1.a	*non modò,*
if I had that leiſure	a. 1.	16.1.b	*si mihi tantũ essetotij*
that you haue,	a. 1.	16,1.c	*quantum est tibi,*
but alſo	a. 1.	16.1.d	*verùm etiam*
if I would ſend as ſhort letters	a. 1.	16.1.e	*si tam breueis episto-las velim mittere*
(as you are wont to doe.)	a. 1.	16.1.f.	(*quod tu soles fa-cere*)
and	a. 1.	16.2.	*&*

Februarij.

* *Quint.*
* *Lucio.*
* Conſulibus

I

I fhould bee much more frequent	a. 1.	16.3.	(a. 1.15.3.a.) *multò effem crebrior*
in writing	a. 1.	16.3.a	*in fcripto*
then you.	a. 1.	16.4.	*quàm tu.*
But	a. 1.	16.5.	*Sed*
to my weighty and incredible affaires may be added,	a. 1.	16.6.	*ad fummas atque incredibiles occupationes meas accedit,*
that I fuffer no letter to come,	a. 1.	16.7.	*Quòd nullam* (a. 1. 16.7.a.) *epiftolam* (a. 1.16.7.b.)*fino* (a. 1. 16.7.c.) *venire,*
from me,	a. 1.	16.7.a	*à me,*
to thee,	a. 1.	16.7.b	*ad te,*
without fome fubiect, and [mine] opinion.	a. 1.	16.7.c	*abfque argumento ac fententia.*
And	a. 1.	16.8.	*Et*
firft of all,	a. 1.	16.9.	*primùm,*
I will lay open to thee that art a Commonwealths-man , that loues thy countrey,	a. 1.	16.10.	*Tibi* (a. 1.16.10.a.) *ciui amanti patriam* (a.1.16.10.b.) *exponam,*
as it behooueth	a. 1.	16.10.a	*(vt æquum eft)*
the matters of the Commonwealth.	a. 1.	16.10.b	*quæ funt in * rep.*
And then	a. 1.	16.11.	*Deinde*

* Republica.

becaufe

178

becaufe	a. 1.	16.12.	*quoniam*
we are neereft vn-to thee in loue,	a.1.	16.13.	*tibi amore nos proximi fumus,*
we will alfo write thofe things of our felues,	a. 1.	16.14.	*fcribemus etiam de nobis ea,*
which we fuppofe, you will not vnwillingly heare of.	a. 1.	16.15.	*quæ fcire te non nolle arbitramur.*
And	a. 1.	16.16.	*Atque*
in the Commonwealth,	a. 1.	16.17.	*in * rep.*
now efpecially,	a.1.	16.18.	*nunc quidem maximè,*
there is a feare of a French warre.	a. 1.	16.19.	*Gallici belli verfatur metus.*
For	a. 1.	16.20.	*Nam*
the *Ædui* are in battell :	a. 1.	16.21.	*Ædui* (a.1.16.21.a.) *pugnant :*
our brethren	a. 1.	16.21.a	*fratres noftri,*
the *Sequani* haue beene put to the worft.	a. 1.	16.22.	*Sequani malè pugnârunt.*
The *Heluetians* are in armes,	a. 1.	16.23.	*Heluetij* (a.1.16.23.a.) *funt in armis,*
doubtleffe,	a.1.	16.23.a	*fine dubio,*
and	a. 1.	16.24.	(a. 1.16.24.a. *què*
make excurfions	a. 1.	16.24.a	*excurfiones* (a.1.16.24.b.) *faciunt*

* republic

into

into the Prouince.	a. 1.	16.24.b	*in prouinciam.*
The Senate hath decreed,	a. 1.	16.25.	*Senatus decreuit,*
that the Conſuls caſt lots for the two Gallia's,	a. 1.	16. 26.	*vt Couſules duas Gallias ſortirentur,*
[and that] there ſhould be taking vp of ſouldiers,	a. 1.	16.27.	*delectus haberetur,*
[and] that there ſhould be no reſpect had of the vacations,	a. 1.	16.28.	*vacationes ne valerent,*
that there ſhould Ambaſſadours bee ſent	a. 1.	16.29.	*legati* (a.1.16.29.a.) *mitterentur*
with authoritie,	a. 1.	16.29.a	*cum auctoritate,*
to goe vnto the Cities of Gallia,	a. 1.	16. 30.	*qui ad. rent Gallia ciuitates,*
and	a. 1.	16. 31.	(a.1.16.31.a.)*què*
ſhould doe their endeuour,	a. 1.	16.31.a	*darent* (a.1.16. 31. a.) *operam,*
that they ſhould not ioyne with the *Heluetians.*	a. 1.	16.32.	*ne ha ſe cum Heluetijs iungerent.*
The Ambaſſadors are [both]	a. 1.	16.33.	*Legati ſunt*
Quintus, Metellus, Creticus,	a. 1.	16.34.	* Q. Metellus, Creticus, *and*

* *Quintus.*

and	a. 1.	16. 35.	&
Luçius Flaccus,	a. 1.	16.36.	* L. Flaccus,
and	a. 1.	16.37.	&
that Lent-Vnguent.	a. 1.	16. 38.	* τὸ ἐπὶ τῇ φακῇ μύρον.
Lentulus, the fonne of *Clodius,*	a. 1.	16.39.	Lentulus Clodiæ, *filius,*
and	a. 1.	16.40.	*atque*
in this place,	a. 1.	16.41.	*hoc loco,*
I cannot let paffe this,	a. 1.	16.42.	*illud non queo præter-ire,*
that	a. 1.	16.43.	*quod*
my lot being the firſt,	a. 1.	16.44.	*cùm* (a. 16. 44. a.) *mea prima fors exiſſet,*
[that was drawne] among the Confulars	a. 1.	16.44. a	*de confularibus*
with one voice,	a. 1.	16.45.	*vna voce,*
a ful Senate thought it fit,	a. 1.	16.46.	*Senatus frequens* (a. 1.16.46.a.) *cenfuit,*
that I ſhould bee kept within the Citie.	a. 1.	16.46.a	*retinendum me in vrbe.*
The fame happened to *Pompeius*	a. 1.	16.47.	*Hoc idem* (a. 1. 16. 47. a.) Pompeio *accidit*
after me,	a. 1.	16.47. a	*poſt me,*

that

* Luchui

* illud in lente vn-guemum.

that wee two fee-med to be retained, [or referued,]	a. 1.	16.48.	*vt nos duo* (a. 1. 16. 48.a.) *retineri videremur,*	
as pawnes of the Commonwealth.	a. 1.	16.48. a	*quafi pignora * reip.*	*Reipublicæ.*
For	a. 1.	16. 49	(a. 1. 16.49.a.) *Enim*	
why fhould I expect the commendations of other men[abroad,]	a. 1.	16.49.a	*Quid* (a. 1. 16. 49. a.) *ego aliorum in me* * ἐπιφωνήματα *exfpectem,*	* acclamationes.
feeing thefe things [come to paffe,] or are bred at home?	a. 1.	16.50.	*cùm hæc domi nafcantur?*	
Now,	a. 1.	16.51.	(a.1.16.51.a.) *Autem,*	
thus goes the City bufineffe.	a. 1.	16.51. a	*Vrbana* (a.1. 16. 51.) *res fic fe habent.*	
The Law for the diuifion of the fields was maynely moued,	a. 1.	16.52.	*Agraria lex* (a.1.16. 42. a.b.) *vehementer agitabatur,*	
by *Flauius,*	a. 1.	16.52. a	*à Flauio,*	
Tribune of the people,	a. 1.	16.52.b	*Tribuno * pl.*	* plebis.
by direction of *Pompeius,*	a. 1.	16.53.	*auctore* Pompeio,	
which had nothing in it that pleafed the people,	a. 1.	16.54.	*quæ nihil populare habebat,*	

befides

befides the di-rector.	a. 1. 19.55.	*præter auctorem.*
I tooke all away	a. 1. 16.56.	(a.1. 15.56.a.) *ego* (a.1.16.56. b.) *omnia illa tollebam,*
from this Law,	a 1. 16.56.a	*Ex hac* (a.1.16.56.) *lege,*
with great fatisfaction of the affembly,	a. 1. 16.56.b	*fecunda contionis voluntate,*
which concerned	a. 1. 16.57.	*quæ* (a. i. 16.57.a) *pertinebant*
the aggreeuances of priuate perfons:	a. 1. 16.57. a	*ad priuatorum incommodum :*
I freed that field,	a. 1. 16.58.	*liberabā agrum eum,*
which was laid common,	a. 1. 16.59.	*qui* (a.1.16.59.a) *publicus fuiffet,*
when *Publius Mucius,*and *Lucius Calpurnius* were Confuls.	a. 1. 16.59.a	P. * Mucio, * L. Calpurnio * Coff.
I confirmed the poffefsions of thofe that followed *Sylla,*	a. 1. 16.60.	*Syllanorum hominum poffeſſiones confirmabam,*
I held the *Volaterani,* and *Artemitani* in their poffeffion,	a. 1. 16.61.	Volateranos, *&* Artemitanos (a. 1. 16.61.a) *in ſua poſſeſſione retinebam,*

*Publio.
*Lucio.
*Confulibus.

whofe

whofe field *Sylla* had confifcated, but not diuided.	a. 1. 16.61.a	*quorum agrum* Sylla *publicârat, neque diuiferat.*
One motion I was not againft,	a. 1. 16.62.	*Vnam rationem non reijciebam,*
that land fhould be bought	16.63.	*vt ager (a.1. 16. 63. a.) emeretur*
with this money that came newly,	a. 1. 16.63.a	*hac aduentitia pecunia,*
which was receiued	a. 1. 16.64.	*quae (a. 1. 16. 64. a.b.) reciperetur*
from the new cuftomes	a. 1. 16.64. a	*ex nouis vectigal i bus*
for thefe fiue yeeres.	a. 1. 16.64.b	*per quinquennium.*
This whole motion the fenate oppofed,	a. 1. 16.65.	*Huic toti rationi agraria fenatus aduerfabatur,*
fufpecting	a. 1. 16.66.	*fufpicans*
that fome new greatnes was fought after, on the behalfe of *Pompeius*.	a. 1. 16.67.	Pompeio *nouam quandam potentiam quaeri.*
on the other fide,	a. 1. 16.68.	(a.1.16,68. a) *verò*
Pompeius leaned	a. 1. 16. 68.a	Pompeius (a.1.16. 68.b.) *incubuerat*

to the putting of the intent of the law in execution.	a. 1. 16.68.b	*ad voluntatem perfe- renda legis.*
But	a. 1. 16.69.	(a.1.16.69.a.) *Autem*
I confirmed the poſſeſſions of all pri- uate men,	a. 1. 16.69.a	*Ego* (a. 1.16.69.b.) *confirmabam omnium priuatorū poſſeſſiones,*
to the great ſatis- faction of thoſe to whom the lands ſhould bee diſtribu- ted.	a. 1. 16.69.b	*magna cum agrario- rum gratia.*
for	a. 1. 16.70.	(a.1.16.70.a.) *enim*
our armie ſo con- ſiſts	a. 1. 16.70.a	*is* (a. 1. 16.70.) *eſt noſter exercitus*
of ſubſtantiall men,	a. 1. 16.71.	*hominum* (a. 1. 16. 71.a.) *locupletium,*
as you your ſelfe know,	a. 1. 16.71.a	*vt tute ſcis,*
I contented the people and *Pom- peius* with the buy- ing,	a. 1. 16.72.	*populo autem,* & Pompeio(a.1.16.72. a.b.) *ſatisfaciebam em- ptione,*
for	a. 1.16.72.a	*nam*
that I deſired alſo :	a. 1.16. 72.b	*id quoque volebam :*

which

which being diligently ordered,	a. 1. 16.73.	*qua conſtituta diligenter,*
I thought	a. 1. 16.74.	*(a.1.56.47.a.) arbitrabar.*
that both the ſinck of the Citie might be cleanſed, and the ſolitude of Italy be filled.	a. 1. 16.74. a	*& ſentinam vrbis exhauriri,& Italiæ ſolitudinem frequentari poſſe*
But	a. 1. 16.75.	*Sed*
all this buſineſſe grew cold,	a. 1. 19.76.	*hæc tota res(a.1.19. 76.a.) refrixerat.*
being interrupted by the warre.	a. 1. 16.76. a	*interpellata bello*
In ſooth	a. 1. 16.77.	*a.1.16.77.a.) ſanè*
Metellus is a good Conſul,	a. 1. 16.77.a	*Metellus eſt Conſul (a.1.16.77.) bonus,*
and	a. 1. 16.78.	*&*
he loues vs very well.	a. 1. 16.79.	*nos admodum diligit.*
That other	a. 1. 16.80.	*Ille alter*
is ſo little,	a. 1. 16.81.	*ita nihil eſt,*
that he cannot deuiſe	a. 1. 16.82.	*vt planè (a.1.16.82. a.) neſciat*
what he ſhall be.	a. 1. 16.82. a	*quid erit.*
thoſe are the occurrents in the Cōmon-wealth,	a. 1. 16.83.	*hæc ſunt in * rep.*

* Republica.

vnleſſe

vnleffe you thinke that this alfo appertaineth to the Common-wealth,	a. 1. 16.84.	nifi etiam illud ad * remp. putes pertinere,	* Rempub cam.
that one *Herennius* hath often attempted,	a. 1. 16.85.	Herrennium *quendam* (a.1.16.85. a.b. c.d.e.f.) *fæpe iam* (a.1. 16.85.g.) *agere cæpiffe.*	
a tribune of the people	a. 1. 16.85. a	*tribunum* * *pl.*	* Plebis.
one of your precincts,	a. 1. 16.85.b	*tribulem tuum,*	
indeede	a. 1. 16.85. c	*fanè*	
a knaue	a. 1. 15.85. d	*hominem nequam*	
and	a. 1. 16.85.e	*atque*	
a beggerly fellow,	a. 1. 16.85. f	*egentem,*	
to make *Publius Clodius* a Plebeian	a. 1. 16.85. g	*de* * P. Clodio *ad plebem traducendo*	* Publio.
This man is often croff'd.	a. 1. 16.86.	*Huic frequenter interceditur.*	
Thefe are all in the Common-wealth	a. 1. 16.87.	*Hæc funt* (a. 1. 16. 87.a.) *in* * *repub.*	
[as I fuppofe.]	a. 1. 16.87. a	*(vt opinor.)*	
But I	a. 1. 16.88.	*Ego autem*	

as

as soone as, on the Nones of December, I had gotten an exceeding and immortalkind of glory	a. 1.	16.89.	*vt femel Nonarum illarum Decembrium (a 1. 16. 89. a.) eximiam quandam atque immortalem glo-*
linked with the enuie and enmities of many,	a. 1.	16.89. a	*riam confecutus fum iunctam inuidi&, ac multorum inimicitijs,*
I ceafed not to negotiate	a. 1.	16.90.	*non deftiti (a.1.16. 90.a.b.) verfari*
with the famecourage I was wont	a. 1.	16.90. a	*eadem animi magnitudine*
in the Commonwealth,	a. 1.	16.99. b	*in * rep.*
and	a. 1.	16.91.	*&*
to maintaine that reputation that I had vndertaken and fet vpon.	a. 1.	19.92.	*illam inftitutam, ac fufceptam dignitatem tueri.*
But	a. 1.	16.93. a	*Sed*
when firft I perceiued the leuity and weakeneffe of the iudgements	a. 1.	16.94.	*pofteaquam primum (a.1.16.94.a.) leuitatem infirmitatémque iudiciorum perfpexi*
by the abfolution or pardoning of *Clodius,*	a. 1.	16.94. a	Clodij *abfolutione,*
and then	a. 1.	16.95.	*deinde*

Republica.

I

I saw our tole-masters to be easily seuered	a. 1.	16.96.	*vidi noſtros publica-nos facile* (a.1.16.96. a.) *diſiungi*
from the ſenate,	a. 1.	16.96.a	*à ſenatu,*
though they were not pulled away		16.97.	*quanquam* (a.1.16. 97.a.) *non diuelleren-tur*
from my ſelfe:	a. 1.	16.97.a	*à meipſo :*
and further		16.98.	*tum autem*
that the bleſſed men openly enuied vs:	a. 1.		*beatos homines* (a.1. 16.99.a.) *non obſcurè nobis inuidere :*
I meane theſe friends of thine that are delighted in fiſh-ponds	a. 1.	16.99.	(*hos piſcinarios dico amicos tuos,*)
I thought	a. 1.	16.100.	*putaui*
it behooued me to ſeeke after grea-ter fortunes and ſtronger guards:	a.1.	16.101.	*mihi maiores quaſ-dam opes & firmiora præſidia eſſe quærenda:*
Thereupon	a. 1.	16.102.	*Itaque*
firſt of all	a. 1.	16.103.	*primùm*
I drew that *Pom-peius* to that minde,	a. 1.	16.104.	*eum* (a.1.16.104.a.) Pompeium *adduxi in eam voluntatem,*
which had beene ſilent	a. 1.	16.104. a	*qui* (a.1.16. 104.b. c.) *tacuerat*

to

too long	a. 1. 16.104. b	*nimiùm diu*
about our busineſſes	a. 1. 16.104. c	*de rebus noſtris,*
that he acknowledged that the ſafety of the Empire and of the world proceeded from me:	a. 1. 16. 105.	*vt* (a1.1.16.105.a. b.c.e.) *mihi ſalutem imperij, atque orbis terrarum adiudicàrit:*
in the ſenate	a. 1. 16.105.a	*in ſenatu*
not once alone,	a. 1. 16.105.b	*non ſemel,*
but often	a. 1. 16.105.c	*ſed ſæpè,*
and	a. 1. 16. 105. d	(a.1.16.105.e.) *qué*
in many words,	a. 1. 16.105.e	*multis* (a.1.16. 105. d.) *verbis ſuis,*
which did not ſo much concerne mee as the Commonwealth	a. 1. 16.106.	*quod non tam interfuit mea* (a.1.16.106. a.) *quàm* ＊ *reip.* ＊ *reipublicæ*
[for theſe things are neither ſo obſcure that they neede teſtimonie: or ſo doubtfull, that they ſhould deſire commendation]	a. 1. 16.106.a	*(neque enim illa res aut ita ſunt obſcuræ, vt teſtimonium, aut ita ſunt dubiæ , vt laudationem deſiderent)*
that	a. 1. 16. 107.	*quòd*
there were certaine wicked men,	a. 1. 16.108.	*erant quidam improbi,*
		who

who thought	a. 1.	16.10 9.	qui (a.1.16.109. a.b. c.) arbitrarentur
I fhould haue fome difference	a. 1.	16.109.a	contentionem fore aliquam mihi
with *Pompeius*	a. 1.	16. 109 b	cum Pompeio,
by reafon of thofe bufineffes,	a. 1.	16.109. c	ex illarum rerum diſſenſione,
I haue ioyned my felfe with this man	a. 1.	16.110.	Cum hoc ego me (a. 1.16.110.a.) coniunxi
in fo great familiarity,	a. 1.	16.110.a	tanta familiaritate,
that both of vs might be	a. 1.	16.111,	vt vterq; noſtrûm (a. 1. 16. 111.a.b.d.) eſſe poſſit.
in our occafions more fafe	a. 1.	16.111. a	in ſua ratione munitior
and more ftrong	a. 1.	16. 111.b	& (a.1. 16.111.c.) firmior
in the Commonwealth	a. 1.	16.111.c	in * repub.
by this vnion	a. 1.	16.111.d	hac coniunctione
but	a. 1.	16.112.	(a.1.16.112.a.) autĕ
The hatreds of the lafciuious and wanton youth,	a. 1.	16.112. a	Odia (a.1.16.112.) illa libidinoſa, & delicatæ iuuentutis,
which were ftirred vp	a. 1.	16.113.	quæ erant (a. 1.16. 113.a.) incitata
againft me,	a. 1.	15.113.a	in me,

* Republic

are

are so mitigated	a. 1. 16.114.	*sic mitigata sunt*
by my courteous carriage,	16.115.	*comitate quadam mea,*
that they all reuerence me onely [or especially.]	a. 1. 16.116.	*me vnum vt omnes illi colant.*
and to conclude	a. 1. 16.117.	(a.1. 16.117.a.)*deni-que*
I do not now proceede seuerely against any man:	a. 1. 16.117. a	*Nihil iam* (a. 1. 16. 117.) *à me asperum in quemquam fit:*
and yet there is nothing that's base or dissolute:	16.118.	*nec tamen quidquam populare, ac dissolu-tum:*
But	a. 1. 16.119.	*Sed*
the whole course of things is so tempered	a. 1. 16.120.	*ita temperata tota ra-tio est*
that I am constant to the Commonwealth,	a. 1. 16. 121.	*vt* * *reip. constanti-am prastem,*
[and] in my priuate affaires I vse a kinde of caution, or diligencie,	a. 1. 16.122.	*priuatis rebus meis* (a.1.16. 122. a. b. c.) *adhibeam quandam cautionem,& diligen-tiam,*
by reason of the weakenesse of those that are good,	a. 1. 16.122.a	*propter infirmitatem bonorum,*

* Republica.

the

the iniquity of ill-willers,	a. 1.	19.122. b	*iniquitatem maleuo-lorum,*
[and] the hatred of the wicked to-wards me,	a. 1.	16.122. c	*odium in me impro-borum,*
And	a. 1.	16.123.	*Atque*
notwithstanding	a. 1.	16. 124.	*(a.1.16. 124.a.)ta-men.*
we are so infol-ded [or lapt] in new acquaintance,	a. 1.	16.124. a	*ita (a. 1. 16. 124.) nouis amicitijs impli-cati sumus,*
that that crafty *Si-cilian Epicharmus* often whispers in mine eares that song of his.	a. 1.	16.125.	*vt crebrò mihi vafer ille* Siculus *insusurret* Epicharmus *cantilenã illam suam.*
Be sober-	a.1.	16.126.	* τῆφι
and	a.1.	16.127.	* καὶ
remember not to beleeue too soone.	a. 1.	16.128.	*μέμνασο απιστειν.
these are the si-newes of wisedome.	a. 1.	16.129.	*ἀρθρα ταῦτα τῶν φρενῶν.
And	a.1.	16.130.	*Ac*
thus see'st thou as it were a kinde of forme of our pro-ceeding and life.	a. 1.	16.131.	*nostra quidem ratio-nis ac vitæ,quasi quan-dam formam (a.1.16. 131.) vides.*
[as I imagine.]	a. 1.	16.131. a	*(vt opinor.)*
but	a. 1.	16.132.	(a.1.16.131.a.) autẽ

Margin notes:
* Sobrius
* &
* Memine non faeilè credere.
* Hi sunt nerui sapi entiæ.

of

Of thy bufineſſe	a. 1.	16.132 a	De tuo (a.1.16.132.) negotio
thou writeſt often vnto me,	a. 1.	16.133.	ſæpè ad me ſcribis,
whereunto we can apply no help at this preſent.	a. 1.	16.134.	cui mederi nunc non poſſumus.
For	a. 1.	16.635.	(a.1.16.135.a.)enim
That decree of the ſenate is made,	a.1.	16.135. a	Eſt (a.1. 16.135.a) illud* S.* C. (a.1.16. 135.b.c.) factum.
by the mayne au- thoritie of the mea- ner ſort,	a. 1.	16.135. b	ſumma pedariorum voluntate,
[and] of none of vs	a. 1.	16.135. c	nullius noſtrûm au- ctoritate
For	a. 1.	16.136.	Nam
that you ſee,	a. 1.	16.137.	quòd (a.1.16.137.a.) vides,
that my name is not thereat,	a. 1.	16.137. a	me non eſſe adſcri- ptum,
you may perceiue	a. 1.	16.138.	(a.1.16.138.a.) in- telligere potes
by the order it ſelfe of the ſenate,	a. 1.	16.138. a	ex ipſo* S.*C. (a.1. 16.138.)
that there was then another buſineſſe in hand:	a. 1.	16.139.	aliam rem tum rela- tam:

*Senatus
*Conſultum

*Senatus
*Conſulto.

But

but	a. 1.	16.140.	(a.1. 16.140.a.)*autem*
this ⌈ particular ⌉ of free people is added,	a.1.	16.140.a	*hoc* (a.1.16. 140.) *de* POPVLIS LIBERIS (a.1.16.140.b.) *additum,*
without cauſe,	a. 1.	16.140.b	*ſine cauſa,*
and	a. 1.	16.141.	*&*
it is ſo come to paſſe,	a. 1.	16.142.	*ita factum eſt,*
by *Publius Seruilius* the ſonne,	a. 1.	16.143.	*à* *P. Seruilio filio,* ¹ P.Publio.
who gaue his ſentence :	a. 1.	16.144.	*qui* (a.1.16.144. a.) *ſententiam dixit:*
in the laſt place	a. 1.	16. 144.a	*in poſtremis*
But	a.1.	16.145.	*Sed*
it cánot be changed,	a. 1.	16. 146.	*immutari* (a.1.16. 146.a.) *non poteſt,*
at this preſent.	a. 1.	16.146.a	*hoc tempore.*
Therefore	a. 1.	16.147.	*Itaque*
the meetings haue now a long time diſcontinued.	a. 1.	16.148.	*conuentus* (a.1.16. 148.a) *iamdiu fieri deſierunt.*
which were wont to be made.	a. 1.	16.148. a	*qui initio celebrabantur.*
I would haue you ſend me word,	a. 1.	16.149.	*Tu* (a.1. 16.149.a.) *velim me facias certiorem,*

whe-

whether you haue, notwithstanding your allurements, drawne any moneyes from the *Sicyonij*,	a. 1.	16.149. a	*si tuis blanditijs tamen à*Sicyonijs *nummulorum aliquid expresseris,*
I haue sent you the Commentarie of my Consulship composed in Greeke :	a. 1	16.150.	*Commentarium Consulatus mei Grece compositum misi ad te :*
wherein,	a. 1.	16.151.	*in quo,*
if there bee any thing,	a. 1.	16.152.	*si quid erit,*
what may seeme to an Attick, to haue but little taste of a Grecian, or a man of learning.	a. 1.	16.153.	*quod homini Attico, minus Grecum, eruditumqué videatur.*
I will not say,	a. 1.	16.154.	*Non dicam,*
that *Lucullus* said vnto you at *Palermo,*	a. 1.	16.155.	*quod tibi* (a. 1. 16. 155.a.) Panormi, Lucullus(a.1.16.156. b.) *dixerat,*
(as I conceiue)	a. 1.	16.155. a	*(vt opinor)*
touching his histories,	a. 1.	16.155.b	*de suis historijs,*

that

that he had there-fore difperfed fome things that were barbarous, and out of vfe [in them]	a. 1. 16. 156.	*fe (a. 1. 16. 156.a.) idcirco barbara quæ-dam, & * σολоικα dif-perfiſſe,;* * obfoleta
that he might more eafily intimate, that they proceeded frō a Romane,	a. 1. 16. 156.a	*quo facilius illas pro-baret Romani hominis eſſe,*
if you finde any fuch thing in me,	a. 1. 16.157.	*apud me fi quid erit ciufmodi,*
it fhall bee vnwit-tingly, and againſt my will.	a. 1. 16.158.	*me imprudente erit, & inuito.*
I will fend you the Latine [worke.]	a. 1. 16.159.	*Latinum (a. 1. 16. 159.a)ad te mittam.*
when I haue ended it,	a. 1. 16.159.a	*fi perfecero.*
Looke for the third Poëm,	a. 1. 16.160.	*Tertium poëma. ex-pectato,*
left I fhould let paſſe any thing that might commend me.	a. 1. 16.161.	*ne quod genus à me ipfo laudis meæ præter-mittatur.*
Heere take heede you fay not,	a. 1. 16.162.	*Hîc tu caue dicas,*
who praifes their father,	a. 1. 16.163.	*τ̔ις πατίρ αινᾶιι :* * quis pa-trem lauda bit $.
for	a. 1. 16.164.	*(a. 1. 16.144.a.)enim*

if

if there bee any thing that ſhould rather be commended amongſt men,	a. 1. 16.164. a	ſi eſt (a. 1. 16. 164.) apud homines quidquam quod potiùs ſit,
let it be commended,	a. 1. 16.165.	laudetur,
let vs bee diſcommended,	a. 1. 16.166.	nos vituperemur,
who doe not rather commend other things.	a. 1. 16.167.	'qui non potiùs alia laudemus.
Though	a. 1. 16.168.	Quanquam
theſe things which we write, are not commendatory, but Hiſtoricall.	a. 1. 16.169.	non * ἐγκωμιαστικὰ ſunt hæc ſed * ἱστορικὰ quæ ſcribimus. * laudatiuā * hiſtorica.
My brother Quintus iuſtifieth himſelfe vnto me	a. 1. 16.170.	Q. frater purgat ſe mihi * Q. Quintus
by letters :	a. 1. 16.171.	per litteras :
and	a. 1. 16.172.	&
he affirmes,	a. 1. 16.173.	affirmat,
that hee hath ſpoken nothing of you to any man that might wrong you.	a. 1. 16.174.	nil à ſe cuiquam de te ſecus eſſe dictum.

But

But	a. 1.	16.175.	*Verùm*
thefe things are with great care and diligence to be treated of by vs at our meeting.	a. 1.	16.176.	*hæc nobis coràm summa cura, & diligentia sunt agenda.*
Now at length come and fee vs.	a. 1.	16.177.	*Tu modò nos reuise aliquando.*
This *Coßinius* feemes to be a very good man,	a. 1.	16.178.	Cofsinius *hic* (a. 1. 16.178.a.)*valdè mihi bonus homo* (a. 1. 16. 178.b. c. d. e.) *visus est,*
to whom I haue giuen letters,	a. 1.	16.178.a	*cui dedi litteras,*
and	a. 1.	16.178. b	*&*
not light-headed,	a. 1.	16.178.c	*non leuis,*
and	a. 1.	16.178.d	*&*
one that loues you,	a. 1.	16.178. e	*amans tui,*
and	a. 1.	16.179.	*&*
fuch an one,	a. 1.	16.180.	*talis,*
as your letters had fignified vnto mee that he fhould be.	a.1.	16.181.	*qualem esse eum tuæ mihi litteræ enuntiarant.*
Farewell.	a. 1.	16.182.	*Vale.*
on the Ides of March.	a. 1.	16.183.	** Idib.* Mart.*

* Idibus
*Martij.

Com-

Comming to Rome,	a. 1. 17. 1.	*Cùm* (a. 1. 17. 1.a.) *me Romam recepiſſem,*
from *Pompeianum,*	a. 1. 17. 1.a	*è* Pompeiano,
on the I I I I. of the Ides of May.	a. 1. 17. 2.	*ad* I I I I. *Id. Maij.*
Our *Cincius* gaue me that letter from thee,	a. 1. 17. 3.	Cincius *noſter eam mihi abs te epiſtolam reddidit,*
which you ſent	a. 1. 17. 4.	*quam tu* (a.1.174.a.) *dederas*
on the Ides of Februarie.	a. 1. 17. 4.a	* *Idib.* * *Febr.*
To that epiſtle I will by theſe make anſwer.	a. 1. 17. 5.	*Ei nunc epiſtolæ litteris his reſpondebo.*
And	a. 1. 17. 6.	*Ac*
firſt of all	a. 1. 17. 7.	*primùm,*
I reioyce,	a. 1. 17. 8.	(a.1.17.8.a.) *lætor,*
that you perceiue what mine opinion is of you,	a. 1. 17. 8.a	*tibi perſpectum eſſe iudicium de te meum,* (a.1.17.8.)
and then,	a. 1. 17. 9.	*deinde,*
that thou waſt moſt moderate	a. 1. 17. 10.	*te* (a.1.17.10.a.b.) *moderatiſsimum fuiſſe*
in thoſe things,	a. 1. 17.10.a	*in his rebus,*

Side notes:
* quartum
* Idus: alij
Ad I I I I.
Id. Maias.

* Idibus
* Februarij.

which

which me thought were more harſhly and vnpleaſing done by vs, and ours, then was fitting,	a. 1.	17.10. b	quæ mihi aſperius à nobis, atque à noſtris, & iniucundius actæ videbantur,
I earneſtly reioyce:	a. 1.	17.11.	vehementiſsimè gaudeo :
and	a. 1.	17.12.	(a.1.17.12.a.)qué
I iudge this to proceed from no meane loue , and from an exquiſite vnderſtanding.	a. 1.	17.12. a	id (a.1.17.12.) neque amoris mediocris, & ingenij ſummi, ac ſapientiæ iudico.
For which cauſe,	a. 1.	17.13.	Qua de re,
ſeeing thou haſt written to me,	a. 1.	17.14.	cùm ad me (a. 1. 17. 14. a.) ſcripſeris,
ſo ſweetly, diligently, officiouſly and courteouſly,	a. 1.	17.14. a	ita ſuauiter, diligenter, officioſè, & humaniter,
that I ought not onely, not to incite you any more thereunto;	a. 1.	17.15.	vt non modò te hortari amplius non debeam;
but	a. 1.	17.16.	ſed
.indeed I could not haue expected ſo great felicitie or courteſie,	a. 1.	17.17.	ne exſpectare quidem (a.1.17.17.a.b.c.) tantum facilitatis, ac manſuetudinis potuero,

[either]

[either]from thee,	a. 1.	17.17.a	*abs te,*
or	a. 1.	17.17.b	*aut*
from any man elſe,	a. 1.	17.17. c	*ab vllo homine,*
I hold nothing more fitting,	a. 1.	17.18.	*nihil duco eſſe commodius,*
than	a. 1.	17.19.	*quàm*
now to write nothing more of theſe buſineſſes.	a. 1.	17.20.	*de his rebus nihil iam ampliùs ſcribere.*
when we ſhall meete,	a. 1.	17.21.	*Cùm erimus congreſsi,*
then	a. 1.	17.22.	*tum,*
if there be any occaſion,	a. 1.	17.23.	*ſi quid res feret,*
We will conferre thereof betweene our ſelues face to face.	a. 1.	17.24.	*coràm inter nos conferemus.*
Touching that you write vnto me	a. 1.	17.25.	*Quòd ad me* (a.1.17. 25.a.) *ſcribis*
of the Commonwealth,	a. 1.	17.25.a	*de * rep.* * *republica*
you diſpute indeed both louingly and wiſely,	a. 1.	17.26.	*diſputas tu quidem & amanter, & prudenter,*
and	a. 1.	17.27.	*&*
your reaſon differs not	a. 1.	17.28.	(a. 1.17.28.a.) *ratio tua non abherret*

from

from my counsell.	a. 1.	17.28. a	*à meis consilijs* (a. 1. 17.28.)
For	a. 1.	17.29.	*Nam*
wee must neither goe backe	a. 1.	17.30.	*neque* (a.1.17.30.a.) *nobis* (a.1.17.30.b.) *est recedendum*
from the state of our dignitie,	a. 1.	17.30. a	*de statu* (a. 1.17.30. b.) *nostra dignitatis,*
neither	a. 1.	17.31.	*neque*
must wee come within the power of another,	a. 1.	17.32.	(a. 1. 17.32. a) *intra alterius praesidia veniendum,*
without our owne forces :	a. 1.	17.32. a	*sine nostris copijs :*
and	a. 1.	17.33.	*&*
the man	a. 1.	17.34.	*is*
of whom you write,	a. 1.	17.35.	*de quo scribis,*
[he] hath nothing generous [in him]	a. 1.	17.36.	*nihil habet amplum,*
nothing excellent,	a.1.	17.37.	*nihil excelsum,*
nothing that is not base	a. 1.	17.38.	*nihil non summissum,*
and	a. 1.	17.39.	*atque*
popular.	a. 1.	17.40.	*populare.*
But	a. 1.	17.41.	*Verumtamen*

my

my confideration was not peraduenture vnprofitable,	a. 1.	17.42.	*fuit ratio mihi for-taſſe* (a.1.17.42.1)*non inutilis,*
to the peace of my times:	a. 1.	17.42.a	*ad tranquillitatem meorum temporum :*
but	a. 1.	17.43.	*ſed*
verily	a. 1.	17.44.	*mehercule*
it was alſo much more profitable to the Commonwealth	a. 1.	17.45.	* *reip. multò etiam vtilior*
than to my felfe,	a. 1.	17.46.	*quàm mihi,*
to haue withſtood the affaults of wicked men againſt me,	a. 1.	17.47.	*ciuium improborum impetus in me reprimi,*
hauing confirmed the wauering opinion	a. 1.	17.48.	*cùm* (a.1. 17.48.a.) *fluctuantem ſententiam confirmàſſem,*
of a man of great fortunes, authority, and fauour;	a. 1.	17.48.a	*hominis ampliſsima fortuna, auctoritate, gratia;*
and	a. 1.	17.49.	*&*
conuerted him to cómend my actions,	a. 1.	17.50.	(a.1.17.50.a.)*ad mearum rerum laudem conuertiſſem,*
from the hope that bad men gaue him.	a. 1.	17.50. a	*à ſpe malorum.*

* reipublicæ.

Which

Which if it had been to haue beene done by me,	a. 1.	17.51.	*Quod si* (a. 1.17.51. a.) *mihi faciendum fuisset,*
with any leuitie,	a. 1.	17.51. a	*cum aliqua leuitate,*
I should haue e-steemed nothing of so great moment :	a. 1.	17.52.	*nullam rem tanti æstimâssem:*
but yet	a. 1.	17.53.	*Sed tamen*
I so carried all bu-finesses,	a. 1.	17.54.	*à me ita acta sunt omnia,*
not that I [should seeme] euer the lighter for assenting vnto [him:]	a. 1.	17.55.	*non vt ego illi assen-tiens, leuior:*
but	a. 1.	17.56.	*sed*
that hee should seeme the grauer, for commanding me.	a. 1.	17.57.	*vt ille me probans, grauior videretur.*
The rest are, and shall bee so handled by me,	a. 1.	17.58.	*Reliqua sic à me agun-tur, & agentur,*
that wee will not doe any thing,	a. 1.	17.59.	*vt non committamus,*
that wee may seeme to haue done those things by chance	a. 1.	17.60.	*vt ea,* (a.1. 17.60.a.) *fortuitò gessisse videa-mur.*
that wee haue done,	a. 1.	17.60. a	*quæ gessimus,*

I

I will not onely neuer forſake thoſe my good men,	a. 1. 17.61.	*Meos bonos viros illos* (a.1.17.61.a.b.c.) *non modò nunquam deſeram,*
whom you intimate vnto me,	a. 1. 17.61.a	*quos ſignificas,*
and	a. 1. 17.61.b	*&*
that lot of defending the Cómonwealth, which thou ſayſt is falne vnto me:	a. 1. 17. 61.c	*eam quam mihi dicis obtigiſſe* * *σωτήριον :*
but alſo,	a. 1. 17.62.	*ſed etiam,*
though I ſhould be forſaken by it,	a. 1. 17.63.	*ſi ego ab illa deſerar,*
yet	a. 1. 17.64.	*tamen*
I will be conſtant in my firſt determination.	a. 1. 17.65.	*in mea priſtina ſententia permanebo.*
Yet,	a. 1. 17.66.	(a. 1. 17. 66. a.) *Tamen,*
I would haue you thinke this,	a. 1. 17.66.a	*illud* (a. 1. 17. 66.) *velim exiſtimes,*
that I keepe this way of the beſt citizens, without either guard or company,	a. 1. 17.67.	*me hanc viam optimatum* (a.1.17.67.a.) *nec præſidio vllo, nec comitatu tenere,*
after the death of Catulus.	a.1. 17.67.a	*poſt* Catuli *mortem.*
For	a. 1. 17.68.	*Nam*

Spartam.

as

as *Rhinton* faith,	a. 1.	17.69.	*vt ait* Rhinton,
as I take it,	a. 1.	17.70.	*vt opinor,*
thefe that are pre-fent are able to doe nothing,	a. 1.	17.71.	ʽὸι μὰν παρ ὑσὶν ἐ ϭιν,
and thofe others haue no care to doe any thing.	a. 1.	17.72.	ʽὸτι δ᾿ὑσὶν μίλιι,
But how much our louers of fifh-ponds enuy me,	a. 1.	17.73.	*Mihi verò vt inui-deant pifcinarij noftri,*
either	a. 1.	17.74.	*aut*
I will at another time write vnto you,	a. 1.	17.75.	*fcribam ad te aliàs,*
or	a. 1.	17.76.	*aut*
I will keep [it] till our meeting.	a. 1.	17.77.	*in congreffum no-ftrum referuabo.*
But	a. 1.	17.78.	(a. 1. 17.78.a.) *au-tem*
nothing fhall draw me from the Court,	a. 1.	17.78.a	*A curia*(a.1. 17.78.) *nulla me res diuel-let,*
either,	a. 1.	17.79.	*vel,*
becaufe it is meete it fhould be fo,	a. 1.	17.80.	*quòd ita rectum eft,*
or	a. 1.	17.81.	*vel*

becaufe

becaufe it falls out beft befitting my ends,	a. 1. 17.82.	*quod rebus meis maxime confentaneum,*
or elfe,	a. 1. 17.83.	*vel,*
becaufe I am well contente d.	a. 1. 17.84.	*quòd* (a. 1. 17. 84.b. a.) *minimè me pœnitet.*
with that efteeme I haue	a. 1. 17.84. a	(a.1.17.84.b.) *quanti fiam*
from the fenate	a. 1. 17.84. b	*à fenatu*
Of the Sicyonij,	a. 1. 17.85.	*De Sicyonijs,*
as I formerly wrote	a. 1. 17.86.	(*vt fcripfi* (a. 1. 17. 86.a.) *antea*)
vnto you,	a. 1. 17.86. a	*ad te,*
there is no great hope	a. 1. 17.87.	*non multùm fpei eft*
in the fenate :	a. 1. 17.88.	*in fenatu:*
for	a. 1. 17.89.	(a.1.17.89.a.) *enim*
there is no man now	a. 1. 17.89. a	*nemo eft* (a.1.17.89.) *iam*
that complaineth.	a. 1. 17.90.	*qui queratur.*
Wherefore,	a. 1. 17.91.	*Quare,*
if that be it you expect,	a. 1. 17.92.	*fi id expectas,*
it will be long :	a. 1. 17.93.	*longum eft :*
ftriue fome other way:	a. 1. 17.94.	*alia via* (a.1.17.94. a.) *pugna:*
if any [way] you can,	a. 1. 17.94. a	*fi qua potes,*

when

when the order was made,	a. 1.	17.95.	*cùm eſt actum,*
there was no notice taken	a. 1.	17.96.	*neque animaduerſum eſt*
to whom the buſineſſe appertained :	a. 1.	17.97.	*ad quos pertineret :*
and	a. 1.	17.98.	*&*
the meaner ſort of ſenators ran headlong in that opinion.	a. 1.	17.99.	*raptim in eam ſententiam pedarij concurrerunt.*
It is not yet time to diſannull the decree of the ſenate :	a. 1.	17.100.	*Inducendi * S. * C. maturitas nondum eſt:* * Senatus * Conſulti
in that there neither are any	a. 1.	17. 101.	*quòd neque ſunt*
which doe complaine,	a. 1.	17. 102.	*qui querantur,*
and	a. 1.	17. 103.	*&*
many are delighted, partly in hatred, partly in the opinion of being iuſt.	a. 1.	17. 104.	*multi partim maleuolentia, partim opinione æquitatis delectantur.*
Thy friend *Metellus* is a worthy Conſul:	a. 1.	17. 105.	*Metellus tuus eſt egregius * Coſ.* * Conſul
one thing I reprehend,	a. 1.	17. 106.	*vnum reprehendo,*

that

that he doth not greatly reioyce.	a. 1.	17.107.	quòd (a.1.17.107.a.) non magnopere gaudet.
that there should be newes out of France of peace	a. 1.	17.107 a	otium è Gallia nunciari,
I beleeue,	a. 1.	17.108.	(a.1.17.108.a.) credo,
he desires to triumph,	a. 1.	17.108. a	cupit, (a.1.17.108. triumphare;
I would hee were more moderate in this,	a. 1.	17.109.	hoc vellem mediocrius,
other things are admirable [in him.]	a. 1.	17.110.	cætera egregia.
But the sonne of Aulus carries himselfe so,	a. 1.	17.111.	Auli filius verò ita se gerit,
that his consulship is no consulship,	a. 1.	17.112.	vt eius consulatus, non consulatus sit,
but	a. 1.	17.113.	sed
the blemish of our great [Pompeius.]	a. 1.	17.114.	Magni nostri* ύ αῶπιον. *macula.
Of my compositions	a. 1.	17.115.	De meis scriptis
I haue sent you my Consulship finished in Greeke,	a. 1.	17.116.	misi ad te Græcè perfectum Consulatū meum.
I haue giuen the same booke to Lucius Cossinius.	a. 1.	17.117.	eum librum * L. Cossinio dedi. *Lucio.

I

I ſuppoſe	a. 1.	17.118.	*puto*
you take pleaſure in my [latin works:]	a. 1.	17.119.	*te Latinis meis deleƈtari:*
but	a. 1.	17.120.	(a. 1.17. 120.a.) *autem*
being a Grecian you enuie this Greeke [worke.]	a. 1.	17.120.a	*huic* (a.1.17. 120. a.)*Græco Græcum inuidere.*
If any man elſe write,	a. 1.	17.121.	*Alij ſi ſcripſerint,*
we will ſend vnto thee:	a. 1.	17.122.	*mittemus ad te:*
but,	a. 1.	17.123.	*ſed,*
beleeue me,	a. 1.	17.124	*mihi crede,*
as ſoone as they redde this of ours,	a. 1.	17.125.	*ſimulatque hoc noſtrum legerunt,*
they are growne flower, I know not how.	a. 1.	17.126.	*neſcio quo paƈto retardantur.*
[But] now	a. 1.	17.127.	*Nunc*
(that I may returne to mine owne buſineſſe)	a. 1.	17.128.	*(vt ad rem meam redeam)*
Lucius Papirius Pætus hath giuen mee thoſe bookes,	a. 1.	17.129.	* L. Papirius Pætus, (a. 1. 17. 129.a. c.)*mihi libros eos*(a.1. 17.129.d.) *donauit,*
a good man,	a. 1.	17.129. a	*vir bonus,*

and

* *Lucius.*

and	a. 1. 17.129.b	(a.1.17.129.c.) *qué*
one that loues vs.	a. 1. 17.129.c	*amator* (a.1.17.129. b.)*nostri.*
that *Seruius Clodius* left [him]	a. 1. 17 129. d	*quōs* * Ser. Claudius *reliquit,* * Seruius.
Cincius your friend hauing told [me]	a. 1. 17.130.	*cùm*(a.1.17.130.a.) Cincius,*amicus tuus, diceret*
that it was lawfull for me by the law *Cincia* to take [or receiue]	a. 1. 17.130. a	*mihi per legem* Cinciam *licere capere,*
I said	a. 1. 17.131.	(a.1.17.131.a.)*dixi*
I would willingly receiue [them,]	a. 1. 17.131. a	*libenter* (a. 1. 17. 132.) *me accepturum,*
if he brought [thē.]	a. 1. 17.132.	*si attulisset.*
Now,	a. 1. 17.133.	*Nunc,*
If you loue me,	a. 1. 17.134.	*Si me amas,*
If you know	a. 1. 17.135.	*si*(a.1.17.135.a.)*scis*
I loue you,	a. 1. 17.135. a	*te à me amari,*
do what thou canst by thy friends, retainers, thine acquaintance, and lastly by thy freeemen and thy seruants,	a. 1. 17.136.	*enitere per amicos, clienteis, hospites, libertos denique, ac seruos tuos,*

that

that there be not so much as a leafe loſt.	a. 1.	17. 136. a	*vt ſcheda nequa depereat.*
For,	a. 1.	17.137.	*Nam,*
I haue great neede both of thoſe Greek bookes and Latine.	a. 1.	17. 138.	*& Græcis his libris,* (a.1.17.138.a.) *&Latinis*(a.1.17.138.b.c) *vehementer opus eſt.*
which I preſume,	a. 1.	17.138. a	*quos ſuſpicor,*
which I know	a.1.	17. 138.b	*quos ſcio*
hee hath left,	a.1.	17.138.c	*illum reliquiſſe,*
For	a. 1.	17.139.	a.1.17. 139.) *autem*
I doe euery day more then other quiet my ſelfe in thoſe ſtudies.	a. 1.	17.139.a	*Ego* (a.1. 17. 139.) *quotidiè magis* (a.1. 17. 139.b.) *in his ſtudijs conquieſco.*
when I can get any time(from my lawbuſineſſe,)	a. 1.	17.139. b	*quod mihi(de forenſi labore) temporis datur,*
Thou ſhalt do me a very, yea, a very good turne,	a. 1.	17.140.	*Per mihi,per,inquam, gratum feceris,*
if thou ſhalt herein be as diligent,	a. 1.	17.141.	*ſi in hoc tam diligens fueris,*
as thou art wont to be in thoſe occaſions,	a. 1.	17.142.	*quàm ſoles in his rebus,*

which

which thou think-eſt I am much deſirous of.	a. 1. 17.143.	*quas me valdè velle arbitraris.*
and	a. 1. 17. 144.	(a. 1. 17. 144. 2.) *qué*
I commend alſo *Pato's* owne affaires vnto thee:	a. 1. 17.144.2	*ipſius* (a.1.17.144.) Peti *tibi negotia commendo*:
for which he giues thee very great thanks.	a. 1. 17.145.	*de quibus tibi ille agit maximas gratias.*
And,	a. 1. 17. 146.	*Et,*
that you wilt now at length come 'and viſit vs,	a. 1. 17. 147.	*vt iam inuiſas nos,*
I do not onely in-treat [thee]	a. 1. 17. 148.	*non ſolùm rogo,*
but I counſell [thee.]	a. 1. 17.149.	*ſed etiam ſuadeo.*

Finis Libri primi Ciceronis ad Atticum.

EXERCISES

out of this former Booke of
Cic. ad *Atticum,* clauſed for the
vſe of our Method.

Auing hitherto giuen the Leſſons of
this booke; we are now to ſet downe
ſome exerciſes promiſed alſo in the
Title.

Theſe exerciſes are of two ſorts. The firſt are
giuen to Schollers at their firſt entrance into our
Schooles, of purpoſe, to trie their preſent abi-
lities.

The ſecond are giuen them within a moneth
after they haue begun to learne by our way of
teaching : that by compariſon made betweene
the firſt, and theſe; the temperate and ſound
man, by taſting either fruite, may rightly iudge
the difference of the trees that bare them.

Both theſe ſorts of Exerciſes, I will heere ſet
downe, as they were written vnder their owne
hands, and deliuered vnto me by their Maſter:
who keepeth them, as well for the iuſtification
of our Method; as of the Schollers profiting, and
of his owne care and induſtrie in teaching them.

A 2   *Exerci-*

Exercises which were made out of their owne abilitie, before they entred vpon our Method, were such as these that follow.

By *C.R.* Nouember 28. 1626. hauing beene at the Grammar Schoole 7. yeares.

1.

By Grammar.

Amice Amantißime

MVlti inueniũtur fauere nobis, quod videtur facere multum pro expedimento negotiorum nostrorum, quia noster aduersator videtur posse ad faciendum multum vocibus. Tuus Auunculus matre obseruat Custodem super omnes alios : sed stetit me & meum fratrem Eduardum in magna consolatione. In uacatione scribam tibi : nam vides adhuc omnia qua conijciantur cuius more sumus,

2.

By Gram.

By *I.G.* Nou. 28. 1626.

VIdetur (Amantißime amice) plurimum facere propter nostrarum rerum expedimentum, quód permulti sint reperti nobis fauere: quippe Aduersarius noster posse videtur quamplurimum in vocibus agere. Auunculus matre super omnes Cancellarium amplectit, Sed mihi stetit & fratri Eduardo in magno Loco : in uacatione ad te scribam. Nam vides, tam longe vt hactenus coniecturis sit in qua procursione sumus.

By *G.G.* Nou. 28. 1626. hauing beene at the Grammar Schoole 6. yeares.

3.

By Gram.

VIdet multum facere propter expedimentum rerum nostrarum, vt plurimi sunt reperti nobis fauere, quoniam

quoniam aduerſarij noſtri plurimum in voces poſſe vi-
dentur. Auuncul° tuus per matre amplectit Cancellari-
um ſupra omnes: Sed me ſtetit & Eduardū fratrem in
magno ſede, in vacatione ad tę ſcribam eatinus vt huc-
uſque coniectus fuerit in qua ordine ſumus.

By *I. W.* Nou. 28. 1626. hauing beene at
the Grammar Schoole 7. yeares.

By Gram.

4.

MVltum *videtur expedimento noſtri negatij face-*
re, quod multi reperti ſunt nobis fauere : quoni-
am noſtri aduerſatores vident peſſe multum vocibus
facere. Patruus per matris axmis, Cancellarius ſupra
omnes alios. eſt : ſed ſtabat me & meum fratrem Ed-
mundum in magno loco, in vacatione ſcribam tibi nam
vides tam longe, vt hactinus quod poſſunt coniecturi
in quo ordine nos ſumus.

By *M. C.* December 4. 1626. hauing beene
at the Grammar Schoole 6. yeares.

5.

By Gram.

VIdetur *faſſere permultus propter expedimentum*
noſtris negotijs inueniunt multi fauere nobis
quia noſter aduerſitas videt poſſe facere multum in vo-
ces tuus Auucclus per matrem laudent cuſtodiem ſuper
omnia ſed ille ſtet me & fratrem Eduardum in magna
opora In vocatione ſcribam apud te enim vides longe
vt hac tenus coniectus eram in qua curſu ſumus.

By *I. F.* Ianu. 16. 1626. hauing beene at
the Grammar Schoole 6. yeares.

6.

By Gram.

MVltum *videtur facere pro expedimento noſtra-*
rum rerum quod plures reperti ſunt nobis fauere,
quia noſter aduerſator videt poſſe multum facere voci-

A 3   bus

kus auunculus tuus per matrem frequetat cuſtodem preter omnes alios ſed me & fratrem meum Edwardum magno loco ſtabat in biſto tibi ſcribam vides enim eouſque coniectum poteſt quo curſu ſumus.

By *S. H.* Feb. 19. 1626. hauing beene at the Grammar Schoole 8. yeares.

7.

PLurimum expedimento rerum noſtrarum facere videtur quod plurimi nos fauere inueniuntur : quia cuus aduerſarius multum facere in ſermonibus poſſe videtur. Auounculus tuus per mamatrem cuſtodem ſalutat pre aliis ſed ſtabat me atque fratrem Iohannem in loco magno. In vocatione ad te ſcribam nam cernes tam longe vt haccine comitietur in quo curſu ſumus.

By *T. N.* Ian. 8. 1626. hauing beene at the Grammar Schoole 5. yeares.

8.

VIdet facere valde multum pro expedimentum noſtrarum rerum quod ſunt multi veniunt fauere nobis quia noſtri aduerſari vides poſſe facere multe vocibus tuus Auunculus per matrem ſolicitat cancellarium ſuper omnes alii ſed ſtat mihi & frater Edwardus maxime loci vocatio ſcribam tibi vides ſic longe vt hactinus coniecturus eſſe quid curſus ſumus.

By *E. C.* Ian. 22. 1626. hauing beene at the Grammar Schoole 7. yeares.

9.

VIdetur facere multum nam expedimentum noſtri ſunt valde multa inuenit nos quia noſter hoſtis videor poſe facere multum in vocis tuus aunculus per matrem obceruo coſtem ſuper omnis aliis at ſtet me &

meum

meum fratrem Eduardum in magno loco in vacatione
cribam ad te nam eousque vt hic inquæ sumus.

By *E. C.* Ian. 22. 1626. hauing beene at the
Grammar Schoole 8. yeares.

10.

By Gram.

Videtur permultum facere pro expedimento no-
strarum occupationum quòd permulti sunt inuenti
fauere nos quia nostrum aduersarium videtur ese posse
multum facere in vocibus, euunculus tuus per matrem
salutat custodem super omnia sed stet me & fratrem
meum Edwardum in magno loco vacatio scribam tibi
nam tam longè quam adhuc coniecturetur in qua ratio
sumus.

SOme other hauing Englishes giuen them,
haue confessed vnder their hands, that they
were not able to translate them into any Latine,
as *T.B.* and *T.R.* of which, the last excuseth himselfe as hauing beene but 4. yeeres at a Grammar Schoole. Yet within a moneth after they
began, he that was least able, made it as the rest
did, by our Method, thus.

Amantissime amice
Nostris rationibus maximè conducere videtur,
plurimos nostros amicos inueniri : quoniam vide-
tur in suffragijs multum posse aduersarius noster. A-
uunculus tuus obseruat Cancellarium maximè: sed, fuit
& mihi & Eduardo fratri magno vsui. Cum à Iudi-
cijs forum refrixerit, scribā ad te: vides enim, quod ad-
huc coniecturâ prouideri possit, in quo cursu sumus, &c.

By our
Method.2
3
4
5
6
7. 8.
9.
10.

Neither

Neither was this onely, Exercife giuen, as their exercife of triall : but thefe alfo following.

By *T.S.* March the 5. 1626.

11.

Expectamus hic te in Ianuario enim egeimus de veniente tuo impigre.circiter placacionē de amico noftro, fum & habeo adeffe femper iudicare inter tu ,enim putamus idpro fitabile, vt effes id nunc apud prolixcem, veniebat ad tranfactorem, circiter negotium, at exiftimo audiuifti , quod auditur effe abficratus rogo quod putares vt amamus tu optime & quod non fui pone manus cum te in quo poteram.

By *M. R.* March 12. 1626. hauing beene at the Grammar Schoole 4. yeares.

12.

Qvantus dolor cæpi propter mortem noftri fratri Philippi ille (habents fieri omnes elaborationes fuas & officia bona pro me).putes. non puto eft etiā turba ad te fed fulfemus id patienter. Charolus labitur legem cum fui fratri Iofephi Waterhoufe & habeo eo fcribents hoc ad te , fi fortaffe poteft pertenere te quifquā velim habere te curare vt valias & ames nos.

By *T. P.* Aprill 2.1627. hauing beene in the Grammar Schoole 5. yeares.

13.

Thomas tenetur contendere cum Iames circum illa quem dicit illum propofiti fallare illum emorat guliclmi feci illa fri antoni fientem ilum cum omne vt fuit magna ratio iam putare fui prefeptoris fed excufauit fe fuper eumdam fortitudinem fuorum infiuilium iuditiorum & Iurauit non eft bene, hic eft omnis vt fum adhuc dicit. Vale.

All

All which and many other Exercifes were, within a fmall time after, by themfelues (made otherwife able by our Method) thus corrected.

11.

By our Method.

NOs hic te ad menfem Ianuariü expectamus, nam, tuo aduentu nobis opus eft maturo. De noftro amico placando, mea intercefsio & eft & fuit parata; fed, audiffe te arbitror, illum effe minus exorabilem. Abs te peto, vt exiftimes te à me fraterne amari; meum ftudium nec tibi defuiffe. Vale.

12.

By our Method.

QVantum dolorem acceperim Philippi fratris noftri morte, cum is omnia fua ftudia & officia in me contuliffet, tu exiftimare potes. Non puto quin tibi quoque id moleftum fit; fed humaniter feremus. Carolus agere cœpit cum eius fratre Iofepho Waterhoufe; & hoc eô adte fcripfi, fi quid forte ea res ad cogitationes tuas pertineret. Velim cures vt valeas, & nos ames.

13.

By our Method.

THomas cum Iacobo contendere exiftimatur de ijs rebus quas eum dolo malo mancipio accepiffe de Gulielmo diceret. Demonftraui hæc Antonio, fimul & illud oftendi, æquum effe de magiftro nunc cognofcere, fed illud fuam regnum iudiciale oppofuit, & induit morbum. Hæc eft adhuc informata cogitatio, Vale.

Stephen Hawkins.

B   So

So likewise were these that follow.

By our
Method.

DE fraterno negotio quod ad me sæpe scripsisti, nihil arbitror esse iam quod laboraret. Nam, quod mihi mandaras, vt primum à tuo digressu Oxoniam veni, confeceram. Quod soror Isabella magnos articulorum dolores habes, magnopere sum commotus, sed consolationem spero Martinum Cosens missurum esse. Tu velim, ea quæ nobis emisse & parasse scribis, vt quam primum habeamus, cures; vehementer enim expecto. Apud patrem recte est; & magnopere confido illum in nostra potestate fore; proinde noli desperare, quin omnia, cum veneris, sanabuntur.

William Gibbes.

By our
Method.

EGo de meis ad te rationibus scripsi antea diligenter; sed, cum & otij ad scribendum plus, & facultatem dandi maiorem habueris, nunquam certior sum factus de negotijs tuis; tametsi, summum me eorum studium teneat. Cum Timotheo sum locutus, is etiam sibi negat quidquam adhuc scriptum esse. Tu modo videto posthac, vt par mihi sis; si rem nullam habebis, quod in buccam venerit scribito. Vale.

Iosephus Waterhouse.

By our
Method.

NOn puto te expectare dum scribam, de sorore tua; quid de te acturus sis, velim cures; & fac nos quamdiligentissime certiores. Dies fere nullus est, quin Auunculus tuus domum meam ventitet, cuius sermonis ris genus tibi notum esse arbitror, sed est miro quodam modo affectus, & mehercule tibi iratus, quod abs te in mensem Quintilem reiecti sumus. Velim cogites, quid agas omnibus de rebus, propterea quod, durius accipere hoc mihi visus est, quam homines belli solent, sed nullam video grauem subesse causam. Tamen tu velim ne praetermittas (quod facere poteris sine molestia tua) venire Idibus Februarij.

G. G.

THus all our Schollers weekely write, and thus they dayly speake : and other Latine then of this kinde, they neither shall, nor can speake or write by our Method. And this is meerely written out of that little habit that they haue made, within the compasse of three or foure moneths (for at this present, the oldest Schoole we haue, is no older;) and that out of this one little booke of *Cicero*. What then may be done by constant industrie in three or foure yeeres, when our Schooles are stronger; not only after this, but any other Author and stile of writing: I dare boldly here Prognosticate, that in halfe the time, and with halfe the cost and labour that habits of speaking and writing haue beene formerly gotten, there shall be such habits knowne in these our parts, as the like were neuer knowne, or heard of in all the world, since Latine ceased to bee a vulgar Language: *Quicquid in oppositum blatiet Lusciosus, Blaesus aut Balbutulus*

B 2   And

And then (when I am in my graue) that loue and care, for which I am now condemned, fhall be commended. And that great and Gracious Prince of ours, which hath not onely diued into the depth and nature of this old-made new found fountaine of cuftome: but hath opened the Rocke where it long lay vfeleffe; and hath licenfed workmen and labourers to conuey the pure ftreames thereof throughout his Kingdomes, fhall be proclaimed *Pater Patriæ*. And that place fhall by all nations be thought happy, from whence this fountaine firft iffued; which I hold onely to prefage fome future greater bleffings to this Kingdome. For as words are but characters and fhadowes of mens conceptions, and thefe conceptions are but right or crooked fhadowes of truthes and realities: fo this purity of thefe words may foretell vs of a future puritie of other arts and knowlodges; and the purity of thefe, bring vs neerer the truthes of things and their realities.

Befides the prefent vfes of this booke, we are yet further to confider, that euery Mafter that would willingly teach this way, cannot be fo neere vs, as to receiue daily inftructions of proceeding by this Method: nor will he be fo perfect in this booke at the firft, as to know readily how to draw Englifhes out of it for the exercifing of his Schollers. And therefore we haue here fet downe 32 Englifhes, whereof you may giue

The

The 1. after they hauè learned the 24. page
or leſſon, & the reſt as they follow in this table.

1. —— —— —— 24.		17. ——————120.
2. —— —— ——— 30.		18. —— —— ——126.
3. —— —— ——36.		19. —— —— —— 132.
4. —— —— ———42.		20. —— —— ——138.
5. —— —— —— 48.		21. —— —— —— 144.
6. —— —— —— 54.		22. —— —— ——150.
7. —— —— ——60.		23. —— —— ——156.
8. —— —— ——66.		24. —— —— ——162.
9. —— —— ——72.		25. —— —— ——168.
10. —— —— ——78.		26. —— —— ——174.
11. —— —— —— 84.		27. —— —— ——180.
12. —— —— ——90.		28. —— —— ——186.
13. —— —— —— 96.		29. —— —— ——192.
14. —— —— ——102.		30. —— —— —— 198.
15. —— —— ——108.		31. —— —— ——204.
16. —— —— —— 114.		32. —— —— ——210.

And after theſe examples, you may gather
ſundry other exerciſes.

Neither haue we onely reſpected the benefit
of abſent Schoolemaſters herein : but we haue
alſo conſidered ſuch as either cannot or would
not go to Schoole, and yet would gladly learne
the Latine tongue, and that purely. To whom,
though I cannot promiſe, that they ſhall ſpeake
it, tone it, and accent it perfectly, without the
helpe of Maſters, by reaſon they ſhall want the
vſe of ſpeaking and hearing others ſpeake that

Language

Language, as it should be : yet it will much better their abilitie for the vnderstanding and the writing of the Language ; and so will euery clause booke that we hereafter shall deliuer to our Schollers.

But to come to our Exercises (which were drawne first in English, by such as practised the Latine by our method) wee are in them to giue the Reader two aduertisements. Th'one about the English, th'other about the Latine in the Margent.

The English in the Margent is the same English that you shall finde in the foregoing clauses, drawne rather to the expression of euery part of those clauses, than for any further vse for that present. For in drawing your Exercises frō those clauses, you may be sometimes forced to an alteration, for ciuilities sake, and to shun a rudenesse in your owne language, as in changing *thou purposest*, for *you purpose* : *thou hast*, for *you haue* : *thou doest*, for *you doe*, and the like. And sometimes you may be vrged to alter, in respect of your owne occasion, as when you are constrained to leaue *Cicero's* names ; either of places, men, or offices. For such names of offices, men, or places, as are proper to your owne, or any other country ; you would write of : as of *London*, for *Roma* ; *Edward*, for *Quintus* ; *Chancellor*, for *Consull* ; or *a mans name*, for *an office* ; or *an office*, for *a mans name*, and the like. All these you shall finde an-

answerable each to other, by their letters.

But the Latine in the Margent hath no letter before it, and is that which should be placed
in your Latine Exercises, in lieu of what was
altered in your Englifh.

And this is done rather for young beginners,
and such as are of small reading in this language, than for thofe that haue imployed two
or three yeeres about it by this method: And
that no longer than till our Supplements shall
be diuulged; whereby they shall not only be
able to make the like alterations of small moment; as of places, offices and the like: but
shall alter whole Claufes, Senfes, and Exercifes
at their pleafure. To which purpofe alfo, with
little direction, our *Entheatus materialis primus*
already diuulged, as a poeticall fupplement for
Hexameter and Pentameter Verfes, may bee
made vfe of, till that Rhetoricall fupplement
may be publifhed.

The first English, whereby they made their fixt [?]
ten Exercifes of tryall before
rehearfed.

IT feemeth to make very much for the furthe-
rance of our affaires, that there are very many
found to fauor vs: becaufe our aduerfary feemes
to be able to doe much in voices. Thine Vncle
by the mother Courts the [a] *Chancellor* aboue
all

[a] L. Domi-
tius.
Cancellarium.

all others ; but hee stood mee, and my brother
b *Edward* in great stead. In the vacation e at *Lon-*
don, I will write vnto thee. For, thou seest, so
farre as hitherto may bee coniectured in what
course we are, &c.

2.

The second, by which they made the thirteenth
Exercise of tryall before mentioned.

a T**Homas** is held to contend with b *Iames* a-
bout those things, which he said, hee of
purpose to deceiue him had bought of c *Willi-*
am. I haue made these respects knowne to d *An-*
thony, shewing him withall, that it was great
reason to thinke now of his Master. But hee
hath excused himselfe vpon that iurisdiction of
his in ciuill iudgements, and hath sworne hee is
not well. This is all that I am hitherto infor-
med. Farewell.

The third, by which they made the eleuenth
Exercise.

W**Ee** looke for you heere in Ianuary. For,
we haue need of your comming betimes.
About the pacifying of our friend, I am & haue
been alwayes ready to arbitrate betweene you.
But I make account that you haue heard, that he
is hardly to be intreated: I desire you that you
would thinke that I loue you as a brother, and
that I haue not been behinde hand with you in
what I was able. Farewell.

HOw much griefe I haue taken through the death of our brother [a]*William*, hee hauing done all his endeuours and good offices for me, you may coniecture. I doe not thinke but it is also a trouble to you : but we will beare it patiently. [b]*Richard* is falne in Law with [c]*Roger Woluerstone* his brother. And, I haue hereupon written this vnto you, if peraduenture it might concerne you any thing. I would haue you be carefull to keepe your owne health, and to loue vs. Farewell.

[a] *Lucian.* *Gulielmi.*

[b] *Cæcilius.* Richardus. [c] *Cauinius Satyrus.* Rogero Woluerstone.

The fifth.

[a] BRother *Iohn*, I would not haue you ouerslip [the occasion.] If you shal finde any thing else that is proper for that place which you wot of; for in this kinde consists my delight, and wee are onely in that place in quiet from all trouble and businesse. I am glad the [b] *Canterbury* purchase pleaseth you, whither I at this present thought to goe. If I euer grow richer, I will garnish [c]*the same;* and the Statua's you sent me heretofore, I will carry all of them into [d] *that place.* Let vs be with all diligence certified how you may helpe vs to make vp our Librarie. Therefore, keepe your bookes (as you haue

[a] *Iohanni frater.*

[b] *Epirotick* Cantuariensem.

[c] *Caiete eam.* [d] *Tusculanum illum locum.*

C   promi-

promifed me) and be not out of hope (when we come to bee at leifure) that I may make them mine. Looke ye now to it, to keepe your owne health, for, in your courtefie we haue placed all hope of our delight. Farewell.

6.

I Cannot think you expect I fhould write vnto you concerning your fifter. What ᵃ *you purpofe* about your felfe, I would haue ᵇ *you* be carefull, and let vs be with all diligence certified. There is fcarce a day [paffeth,] but ᶜ *your vncle* comes often to my houfe, whofe manner of fpeech I fuppofe you know. But he is wonderfully troubled ; and indeed angry with you, that ᵈ *you haue* put vs off till Iuly. I would haue you bethinke your felfe what ᵉ *you do* about all matters; by reafon that this hee feemes to mee to take worfe than men of a faire condition are wont ; but I fee no caufe of moment to ground vpon. I hold it beft therefore fo farre forth as ᶠ *you can*, without ᵍ *your* owne preiudice, that ʰ *you fhould* come as ⁱ *you haue* appointed on the eight of the Kalends of December. Farewell.

7.

WHeras you write touching ᵃ *your brothers* caufe : Verily, I am of opinion that now there is no need that he fhould take any farther care.

care. For as ſoone as I came to ^b *Cambridge* after your departure, I omitted not [thoſe things] which were to be ſpoken. That your ^c*ſiſter Iſabella* hath great paines of the ioynts, I am much moued; But I hope ^d *Martin C.* will ſend ſome comfortable meſſage. I would haue thee preſently ſend thoſe things which thou writeſt thou haſt bought and prepared for vs; For I am poſſeſſed of an exceeding deſire to haue them. All goes well with [your] ^e *Father*; but I feare that he is grieuouſly offended. Yet be not out of hope, for theſe things will bee remedied when you come. Farewell; on the Ides of February.

8.

^a **A**NTHONIE,
  I charge you in any caſe, that you get mee that helping hand of our friend *the* ^b *Sheriffe*. For I haue a ^c *ſeruant*, in ſooth a wicked fellow, I meane ^d *Roger* your ^e *Couſin-Germane*, and ^f *compa-nion*. I make account you haue heard that the fellow is with ^g *Gregory* th'*Apothecarie*. I wrote ſuch Letters vnto him, whereby I might reprehend him as in an errour, and aduiſe him as ^h *my friend*. But when I had done all I could, it is incredible how much I finde him more obſtinate and confirmed in this ⁱ *wickedneſſe*. The buſineſſe is of that nature, that I cannot with my reputation defend the man, and hold my eſteeme

C 2   either

Marginal notes:

b *Rome.*
Cantabrigiam

c *Terentia.*
ſoror Iſabella.

d *L. Sauſeius.*
Martinum C.

e *mother.*
patrem.

8.

a *Antoni.*
b *Pompeius.*
Vicecomitis.
c *Slaue*
made free.
Famulum.
d *Hilarum.*
Rogerum.
e *Auditor.*
patruelem.
f *retainer.*
Contubernalem.
g *Antonius.*
Gregorio
Pharmacopolâ.
h *my Iunior.*
amicum.
i *indignation.*
nequitiâ.

either with such as are good,or with the people.
Therfore remoue that knaue from thence,if you
can by any meanes. And what thou doest about
all matters,let vs be with all diligence certified.
Farewell.

9.

9.

* *Henriæ*
frater charif-
fimo.
a *Of Publius*
Clodius.
Alexandri.
b *2400. Se-*
ftertij.
Librarum
mille qua-
dringenta(or)
lb cıɔcccc.
c *for L.*
Cincius.
Bartholomæo.
d *Senatu.*
Chriftophero.
e *To the
Common-
wealth.
tuis amicis.

f *Epiftle.*

***D**Eare *Brother Henry*:
Being led by the friendſhip of ª *Alexan-*
der, I haue procured ᵇ *a thouſand, foure hundred*
pounds ᶜ *for Bartholomew,* as you wrote vnto mee ;
not without the murmuring of ᵈ *Chriſtopher,*
From whom thou need'ſt feare no ill,becauſe he
dares not ; thou canſt hope for no good e *to thy*
*friends,*becauſe he will not. But whether he will
or no, I am by this meanes free'd from obſer-
uing a peruerſe man. Yet,about the reconciling
you each to others ancient fauour (if you ſhall
thinke [him]worth it)I promiſe thee,I will both
doe it more induſtriouſly , and I will vrge him
with greater vehemency,than you would haue
me. Although queſtionleſſe he hath ſomething,
which neither thy ᶠ *letter,*nor the commiſſion we
had from thee,can ſo well put out , as you may
take it away by your preſence , with that familiar countenance of thine, if you will bee as
courteous as you were wont to be. In whether-
ſoeuer the fault be, I feare in good earneſt, that
this will feſter further that is infeɕted. Therefore, in reſpeɕt of this my doubt (as you haue
appointed)

appointed) be fure, that you be ^g at *Canterburie* g At Rome
Cantuaria.
on the Kalends of Ianuary : becaufe I confi-
dently beleeue, that he will doe as hee fhould,
and as we would haue him. Farewell.

10.

10.

I Haue not thought it troublefome, at this
prefent, to write vnto thee ; that it is a matter
of great infamie, that thy familiars nobly def-
cended, ^a *fhould* be aduerfaries to our honour ; a will.
but, we will beare it patiently. I fuppofe, that
there is nothing more purfued, now, ^b *at Paris*, b at Rome.
Parifijs.
at leaft among the Citie-competitours, with all
iniuries, than thofe that ftand to be Magiftrates:
Therefore, we muft haue recourfe to ^c *the Earle* : c *Confidius,*
&c.
Comitem.
it is manifeft that ^d *he* beares vs great affection; d *Pompeius.*
illum.
and, moreouer, *the* ^e *treafurer* beares the fame e My brother
Quintus.
Thefaurarius.
minde towards ^f *our vncle*, that wee would haue f *Pomponia.*
auunculum.
him, as I fuppofe. Therefore, we will vfe all di-
ligence, in this bufineffe. I would haue you ^g *doe* g Vfe.
your beft endeuour, that you examine the whole
matter how it ftands. Farewell.

11.

11.

B Y the enticement ^a *of a certaine Lawyer*, I haue a Of the
Conful
Pifo.
iurifconfulti
cuiufdam.
formerly written vnto you, concerning the
order proclaimed on the very Market day. But
the fame day I was fo hindred by imployments,
that you may accufe mee of negligence in wri-

C 3　　　　　　ting

ting letters. But now I haue added something, ^b *yet* so, that it may be wel perceiued, nothing [is done] in sinceritie, nothing nobly. For things stand ^c *as* you left them. But of these things I will write more particularly hereafter. Concerning my brother, I think we must haue recourse to ^d *the Archbishop,* ^e *Treasurer,* [and] ^f *Chancellor,* but I durst not say [so much] before, because I beleeue that you haue heard that the matter was referred to the ^g *Iudges,* and the ^h *High Sheriffes.* At this time I haue nothing else to write vnto you. Farewell.

12.

I Feare, it may proue distastefull to write vnto thee, how full of businesse I am at this present. But yet indeed, I was so hindered by imployments, that I haue scarce time to write this little letter, and that (time which I had, was) stolne from affaires of greatest importance. So that I was much troubled when I wrote; and therefore this very letter is [^a *the*] *shorter.* But hereafter, when we come to be at leisure, ^b *expect* a large letter from vs. But howsoeuer, vnderstand thus much, ^c *our aduersarie* himselfe ^d [*is*] of a weake and wicked spirit, onely a wrangler. Yet thou needst feare no ill, ^e [*I*] *hauing* formerly signified vnto thee by letter, that I could doe what wee desired with him. And this was almost all I had to say vnto thee. Farewell.

I

Marginal notes:

b *but*

c *so as.*

d *Considius. Archiepiscopum.*
e *Axius. Thesaurariu.*
f *Selicius. Cancellarium.*
g *Virgins. Iudices.*
h *Pontifices. vicecomites.*

a *shorter.*

b *(and)expect.*

c *the Consul. Aduersarius.*
d *of.*
e *hauing.*

I Make account that you haue heard, that I haue sent my freed slaue the Keeper of the common gaine; Know'st thou whom I meane? I meane a *Richard* your auditour and retainer, of whom you wrote vnto me. Concerning him, b *Iohn the Merchant* sends mee word, that he reproachfully iniuried c *Adrian, Horatio, Gregorie, and Alexander the Gouernour*. And d *Henry* writes he heard these things. In good earnest, I am much disturbed, for the familiaritie of e *Adrian,* himselfe: for, it is manifest that f *he* beares g *me* great affection. Vnderstand thus much, that the fellow is with *Anthony*. Therefore, remoue that knaue from thence, if you can by any meanes. For, indeed, I desire it should be so. I would haue you vse your best endeauour in this businesse; and let vs be with all diligence certified. Farewell.

14.

I Haue formerly written to you of mine owne occasions diligently. But, though a *you haue* both more leisure to write, and better meanes of sending; yet, I neuer was certified, from b *you*, about the affaires I gaue you in charge. I haue spoken with c *Timothy*, and, he denies that any thing hath been written to him. Looke you

now

now to it, that you equalize me, in performing the part d *of a brother*. If you shall haue nothing, write whatsoeuer comes into your minde. Farewell, on the Kalends of Ianuary.

d of a candidate. fraterno,

15.

I Much desire to know, what fell out, about the affaires that I gaue you in charge ; for, from the time a *you went* b *from London,* c *you wrote* nothing, about those things, to mee. Take heed you promise not your Librarie to any man: for in d *it* wee haue placed all hope of our delight ; and, if c *you can* finde any ornaments that are proper for the Academie, or, whatsoeuer you shall haue of that kinde, that is proper for that place, make no difficultie to send it ; for, in this kinde consists my delight. I haue nothing else to write vnto you. Farewell.

a thou went'st. b from Brundusium, Londino. c thou wrot'st. d thy courtesie. illd. e thou canst

16.

WHat should be attempted, about the pacifying of our friend, or, about the reconciling you each to others ancient fauour; I thought fit to be determined, according to your owne pleasure. But, I make account that you haue heard , that hee is hard to bee intreated: Moreouer, hee is of so wicked a minde through the habit of vice, that hee hath begun to hate a *vertue*. When I shall perceiue how b *you are affected,* then I shall know, what I am to goe vpon.

a Pompeius. virtutem. b The Nobles are affected. voluntatem tuam.

In

In the meane while I desire you, that you bee at
ᶜ *Cambridge,* on the Ides of February. Farewell.

17.

COme at length to see how wee doe, if you
can by any meanes; or, if you will bee as
courteous as you were wont to be. And, what
fell out, concerning your sister,ᵃ *of whom* I know
you very carefull, when you come, you shall
know of mee. Wee looke for you here in Ia-
nuarie; wherefore, let vs bee with all diligence
certified how long ᵇ *you will* abide in ᶜ *France.* If
I euer grow to be richer, I will garnish ᵈ [*my*]*Li-*
brarie; I keepe all the little things that I haue
gathered together to that purpose; for, in this
kinde consists my delight. Things stand so, as
you left them. All goes well with [your] ᵉ *sister,*
and wee haue a care of her; but know, your
grandmother is dead, out of a desire to see
ᶠ *you:* But, these things will be remedied, when
you come. Farewell.

a whereof.

b thou wilt.
c *Epirus.*
Galia.
d *Caieta.*
Bibliothecam.

e mother.
(or oræns.

f thee.

18.

ᵃ YOu *demand* of me, what ᵇ*Philips* first speech
was, concerning the law proposed in the
ᶜ *Parliament House.* This was the matter [of ᵈ*his*
discourse:] That the ᵉ *Iudges* should exhort the
people, to accept of the law [or sentence.] I being asked mine opinion, spake many things,
                    D   about

a thou de-
mandest.
b *Pompeius.*
Philippi.
c Senate.
comitijs.
d my.
e Consuls.
Iudices.

f Senate.
Comitia,

g Rome.
Parisienses.

h thou doft.
i thou pur-
pofeft.
k thee.

a to the
Common-
wealth.
illi.
b thou
need'st.

about the Commonwealth, not pleafing to fuch as were in miferie, not gratefull to the happy. I recalled *the* f *Parliament* to their wonted feueritie, both, with a continued fpeech, [and] very full of grauitie. If euer I did abound in arguments, [it was] at that time. You haue vnderftood the affaires of g *Paris* : Now, I defire, you would let mee vnderftand, what fell out about thofe things, about which you wrote vnto me, and, what h *you doe*, what i *you purpofe* to doe, let me heare from k *you*, very diligently. Farewell.

19.

WHat newes fhall I write you ? what [is there any ?] Yes [there is.] The bloud of enuie hath beene drawne, and, with fo great a wound giuen a *thereunto*, that b *you need* feare no ill. And, yet, griefe is falne vpon good men, vpon what fufpitions, verily, I know not. But, which is more then all the reft, [their] vertue is no whit leffened. Wherefore, I hope, that all things ftand fo, as I defired & laboured they fhould. Now, becaufe wee haue beene alwayes both moft defirous of praife, and wee haue vndergone the hatreds and enmities of many, for the Commonwealths fake, we will, vfe all diligence, that wee may be commended, and beloued of all men: For, in this kinde, wee are fo carried away with defire, that wee pleafe our felues. Farewell.

I

20.

I Was much troubled when I wrote, in that, I neither had the opportunitie, to haue men that are to ^a *goe* to ^b *Cambridge*, neither did I well know, what to giue. And further, I was vnwilling, that that kind of familiar speech of ours should come into the hands of strangers: For I was neuer certified from thee, that there was any messenger. Whereunto may be added, that I haue not knowne, where thou wast. Wherefore, in respect of this my doubt, I wrote but seldome to ^c *thee* heretofore. When ^d *thou remainest* certaine in any place, then shall I know, what is to be done. I charge ^e *thee* in any case, to keepe thine owne health, and to loue vs. Farewell.

a come.
b Rome.
Cantabrigiam.

c you.
d you remaine.

e you.

21.

MY brother ^a *Matthew* beares the same minde towards ^b *your daughter*, that we would haue him ; which I did not looke for, and, which I saw you also suspected vpon your departure from vs. There are many tokens thereof, [and] this is not the least, that, he was now with her at the ^c *countrey Mannour*. Therefore, I trust, that he will doe as he should, and, as we would haue him. In this businesse ^d *Robert* laboureth, and he is earnest, that it might be so.

a *Quintus*, *Mathæus*.
b *Pomponia*, *filiam tuam*.

c Mannour of *Arpinas*, *rustico prædio*.
d *Pistr*: *Robertus*.

Where-

Wherefore, concerning my brother, I truſt, that all things ſtand ſo, as I deſired and laboured they ſhould. But howſoeuer, I will vrge him with greater vehemencie, becauſe by your letters I perceiue you haue ſo great a will thereunto. Farewell.

22.

22.

HAuing formerly ſignified vnto thee by letters, how full of buſineſſe I am, I cannot thinke you expect I ſhould write vnto you: Wherefore, left *a you ſhould* wonder, I haue hereupon written this vnto b *you*, if peraduenture it might concerne you any thing. c *Antonie* that friend of ours is angry with you; vpon what ſuſpitions, I can more eaſily imagine, than write: and, I doubt not, but report will ſooner relate this vnto you, than any of our letters: Be reconciled with d *him*, if you can by any meanes; or, if you ſhall thinke [him] worth it. When we come to be at leiſure, looke for often letters from vs. Farewell.

a thou
ſhould'ſt.
b thee.
c *Cæcilius.*
Antonius.

d *Luccinus.*
illo.

23.

23.

COntinuing my purpoſe and appointment, concerning your ſiſter, I haue giuen order to a *Richard*, that he b *ſhould* purchaſe the Cæcilian houſe, on c *my* behalfe, which I will giue to d *your ſiſter her ſelfe*, as the gods ſhall helpe mee.

a *Titius.*
Richardo.
b *might.*
c *your.*
meae.
d *Quintus*
himſelfe
ſuori.

mee. For, in ^c *her* courtefie wee haue placed all
hope of our delight, which we meane to haue.
And, in good earneft, we are fo carried away
with defire, that we are by ^f *you* to be furthered
[therein,] Wherefore, concerning your fifter,
let vs be with all diligence certified; if you will
be as courteous as you were wont to be; and
endeuour with diligence and effect, that we
may be commended and beloued of ^g *her.* Farewell.

e thy.
us.

f thee.

g him.
ed.

24.

24.

WEe looke for you here in Ianuary, if
^a *you can,* and, indeed, we haue neede
of your comming betimes : For, there is not
a man, efpecially at this prefent, with whom I
may communicate. Wherefore, I defire thee,
and our difcourfes : for, we are vnited together with much and pleafing familiaritie; and,
in good earneft, in fuch fort, that I thinke that
wee ought to tolerate any inconueniences,
vices, or iniuries that fhall fall out amongft vs.
Therefore, come at length to fee how we doe,
if you will be as courteous as you were wont
to be. For, I want nothing more at this prefent, than that man, with whom I might con-
uerfe. Farewell.

a thou canft.

D3

25.

I Haue very well perceiued a *thy* forrowings and ioyings, in the diuerfities of my fortunes; wherein, I did not onely defire thy prefence, to counfell me, but alfo to be a fpectator of mine admirable encounters. But now, the Commonwealth is afflicted, by a notable departure of the good men, by bought and defiled iuftice; which I defiring to remedie, I vfed all the powers of my minde and wit. But, thou demandeft of me, that I fhould now returne to priuate affaires, as thou doeft. A certaine ambition led me to the defire of honour, and fome other reafon not to be blamed, led thee to an honeft leifure. Therefore, I cannot blame b *thy* determination, in that caufe. I will againe doe mine endeauour, and, thefe things will be remedied, as I hope; and, as I defired and laboured they fhould. Farewell.

26.

I Muft earneftly requeft you to pardon mee for one thing, which if I compaffe, I am richer then *Craffus*. There is one a *William*, who, b *demanded* of bb *mee*, on your behalfe, to appeare for him againft c *Iofeph*. I reprehended d *him*, and, I faid, in this bufineffe, that

Marginal notes (left column):

a your.

b your.

a *C. Heren-nius. Gulielmus.*
b *he demanded.*
bb *him.*
me.
c *Satyrus. Iofephum.*
d *the Senate. illum.*

c I

e *I was* to be pardoned, hee hauing done all his endeuour, and good offices for me: Moreouer, it is manifeſt that f *hee* beares g *mee* great affection. For, wee are vnited together with much and pleaſing familiaritie. Therefore, I haue made theſe reſpects knowne h *to you*, and I truſt, that I haue iuſtified my cauſe vnto you, if you will be as courteous as you are wont to be. When I know what account you make hereof, then I will write more vnto i *you* concerning theſe matters. Farewell.

e *I am.*
f *Pompeius, illum.*
g *vs, mihi.*
h *vnto Cæsilius, tibi.*
i *thee.*

27.

I Much deſire to know, what fell out, that the annuall Feaſts of a *Saint George* ſhould not be celebrated. I feare, that ſome inconuenience may riſe thereby. Yet, ſo farre as hitherto, may bee coniectured, I will giue b *thee* a glimmering of it. There is feare of a French warre, and, there are many tokens thereof, this is not the leaſt, that, there ſhould bee taking vp of ſouldiers, in all places. It is incredible, how this fire firſt fell, nor as yet, will I lay [it] open to thee, that art a Commonwealths man, that loues thy conntrey; neither will I commit c [*it*] to this Epiſtle: For, I dare not truſt letters, in which I am a little freer then ordinarie, neither, d *with vnknowne Merchants*, nor e *with Carriers*. Therefore, I will more commodiouſly explaine

a *Of the youth. Sancti Georgij.*
b *you.*
c *(them.)*
d *with men of Achaia. ignotis mercatoribus.*
e *Of Epirus. tabellarijs.*

plaine the mischiefe of all this businesse vnto
^f *thee* at our meeting. Farewell.

^f you.

28.

28.

THere are many things, since thou went'st
from me, which vexe and trouble mee;
and, in good earnest, in such sort, that I
had scarce time to write this little letter. I
haue tryed all things, which concerned the
aggrieuances of priuate persons; but, where
the fault of this inconuenience resteth, verily, I know not. Wherefore, I desire you
that you would come speedily, who ^a *art
wont* to bee vnto mee priuie to all my priuate businesse. For, neither my paines, nor
quiet, nor businesse, nor leisure can longer
want thy most sweet, and louing counsell,
and discourse. But, these things will easily
bee mitigated, as I suppose, when you come.
Farewell.

^a wast.

29.

29.

AS sooner as I came to ^a *London*, after
your going hence; the seruant sent by
your sister ^b *from Cambridge*, gaue mee a letter that came from you. Therefore, that I
^c *may write* something in answer of your let-
ter; Vnderstand thus much, that there are

^a Rome.
Londinum.

^b from
Rome.
Cantabrigiâ.

^c wrote.

ver

very many found to fauour vs, in the occasion of our petition. When I shall perceiue how the Nobles are affected, vpon such an occasion, then I shall know, doubtlesse, what I am to goe vpon. In the meane while, I will looke to the mayne chance, and, in the vacation d *at London*, I will write more vnto thee concerning these matters. Farewell. On the Ides of February.

d at Rome. *Londini.*

30.

30.

YOur letters are brought vs too-too seldome, I hauing reputed the hearing of them no trouble. I haue formerly written to you of mine owne occasions diligently, not once alone, but often, verily : And, if I had that leisure to write backe againe, that you haue, in this kinde, I should bee much more frequent, then I was wont. Concerning your sister, b *of whom* I know you are very carefull, I had rather c *your Vncle* should giue d *you* counsell by letters than my selfe. What fell out, about e *the fight at Sea*, at this present, I will not say, neither will I commit [it] to an vnknowne messenger. Farewell. On the Kalends of December.

b whereof.

c *Peduceus, auunculum.*
d thee.

e the iudgement,
bello nauali.

E   Whereas

WHereas you write, about the appeafing of our friend, or rather about the full reftoring him [vnto thee] I haue tryed all things; but, 'tis wonderfull, how much I finde him more obftinate and confirmed, in that wayward fafhion; than men of a faire condition are wont. On the other fide, how much courtefie is in my brother a *Iofeph*! how b *ftout* a Souldier! not onely, in performing the part of a c *brother*, but alfo d *in maintaining* that reputation that I had vndertaken, and fet vpon. Indeed, he hath no man like him. I haue nothing elfe to write vnto you, onely [thus much,] that you efteeme fo much of our loue, that we may forthwith fee you. Farewell. On the eleuenth of the Kalends of Februarie.

32.

MEn are of an affured opinion, that there fhould be newes out of France of Peace, and, that the Embaffies fhould bee deferred alfo. Therefore, when this fhall publikely bee reported, then indeed will a *the Englifh* very willing ioyne b *themfelues* with the c *French*. There's great fuite made : But, there is one d *Iohn Galatine* amongft the Magiftrates, who gaue his fentence, that it was more fit to deftro,

ſtroy all things, than to thinke of e *peace* already. I doubt not, but report will ſooner relate
this vnto you, then any of our letters. Come
at length to ſee how wee doe : In the meane
while, when we come to be at leiſure, we will
ſend vnto f *you.* Farewell. On the Nones of
December.

e an Ouer-
ſeer.
part.

f *thee.*